British Columbia

ANTHONY HOCKING

Publisher: John Rae

Managing Editor: Robin Brass

Manuscript Editor: Jocelyn Van Huyse

Production Supervisor: Lynda Rhodes

Graphics: Pirjo Selistemagi

Cover: Brian F. Reynolds

THE CANADA SERIES

McGRAW-HILL RYERSON LIMITED

Toronto   Montreal   New York   St. Louis   San Francisco
Auckland   Bogotá   Guatemala   Hamburg   Johannesburg
Lisbon   London   Madrid   Mexico   New Delhi   Panama
Paris   San Juan   São Paulo   Singapore   Sydney   Tokyo

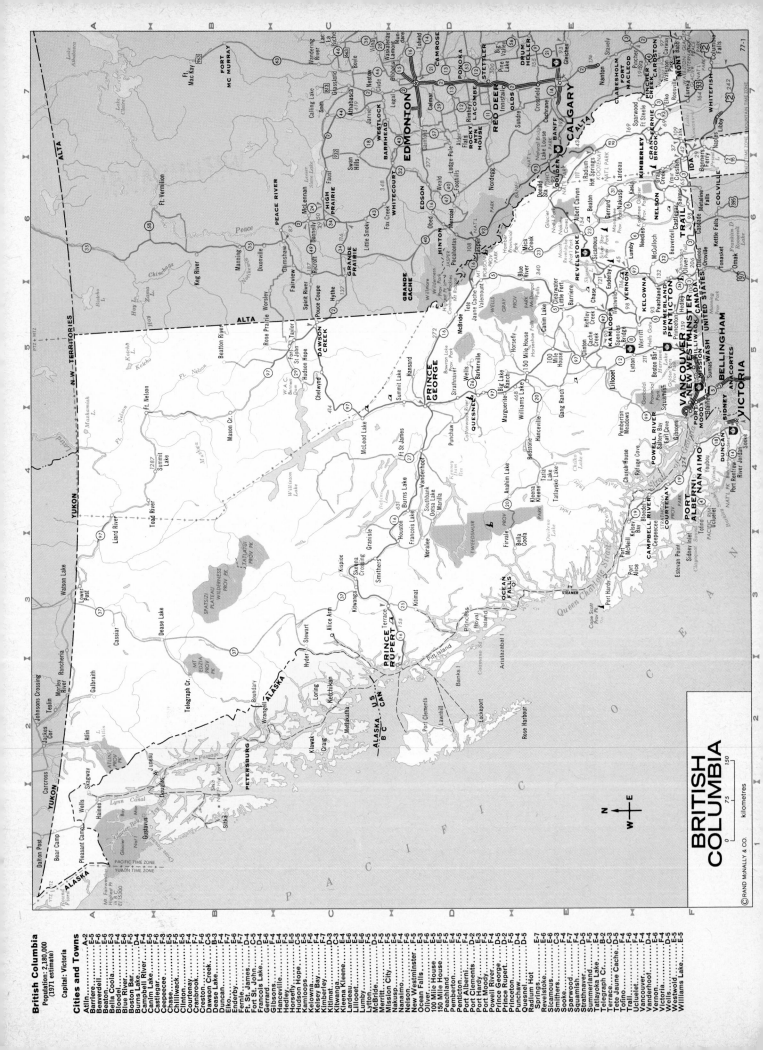

CONTENTS

BRITISH COLUMBIA

British Columbia is named after a river, which in turn is named after a ship. The original *Columbia* was from Boston and took part in the Pacific sea otter trade of the 1780s and 1790s. Her captain discovered the river's estuary in 1792.

Until 1846, the river served as the boundary between British and American territory. Then the international border was redrawn along the 49th parallel to the north, allowing for an eccentric kink southwards to accommodate Vancouver Island. Only the upper reaches of the Columbia river could still be called British.

B.C.'s northern boundary runs along the 60th parallel, but again there is an eccentricity. From 54°40′ northwards the coast belongs to Alaska, according to a treaty of 1825 signed by Britain and Russia. In the east, B.C. adjoins Alberta, in part along the 120th meridian and in part along the height of the Rocky mountains.

All told, British Columbia is Canada's third-largest province, almost all of it a wilderness of rivers, forests, and mountains little disturbed even by resource industries. Both inland and on the coast, its scenery dazzles visitors and provides exquisite settings for a rich diversity of wildlife.

Forestry, mining, tourism, and manufacturing are B.C.'s leading industries, and agriculture and fishing are important, too. They are shared by a population drawn from all over the earth, not least the descendants of the original inhabitants and many whose ancestors lived in Asia.

Several ranges of mountains separate most British Columbians from their fellow Canadians, and they look to the Pacific rather than towards the St. Lawrence. Few seem to regret the isolation, but those who do are compensated by a leisured lifestyle that works wonders for both body and mind.

Water sports are a way of life on Canada's west coast, and thousands of B.C. families own sailing boats or motor cruisers for use throughout the summer.

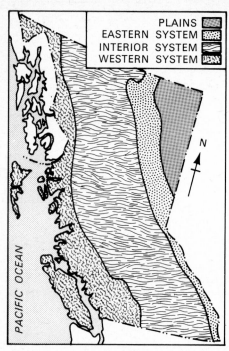

Three systems of mountains comprise the Canadian Cordillera, part of the chain that extends from Alaska to the south of South America. In the north-east is a portion of the great plains of Canada's interior.

THE CORDILLERA

North-eastern British Columbia is a section of the great plains of North America, sediments that were once at the bottom of ancient seas and freshwater lakes. The remainder forms part of the chain of mountains that extends from Alaska to the tip of South America — as the Spanish termed it, the Cordillera.

Geologists divide and subdivide the Cordillera into what seems an infinite number of systems, but in B.C. they fall into three main groups. In the west are the mountains of the coast and the large offshore islands, in the east are the famous Rockies, and in the middle are the mountains and plateaux of the interior.

In the past, geologists have had to treat each of these groups as a separate entity. They understood when and how the various mountains were formed, but not the connections between them. Recently earth scientists have taken a fresh look at the Cordillera in the light of a startling new theory.

According to these scientists, the earth's crust consists of seven large, rigid plates and a number of smaller ones. Some of the plates consist of a single layer of dense basalt about 10 km thick, exposed on the ocean floor. In other cases the basalt is topped by lighter granitic formations up to 35 km thick — the continental land masses.

Like the skin on hot soup, the plates float on plastic magma that forms the earth's mantle. Over the years there are changes in the mantle, and the plates slowly respond and move into new positions. This may cause earthquakes, as when the plates slide past each other, or more drastic consequences if they collide or pull apart.

As plates part company, basalt volcanoes from the mantle fill the rift. When the plates collide, they may buckle and fold the continental mass, or one plate may ride over the other. In that case the first plate is levered upwards, and the other is pushed into the mantle and melts, setting off a volcanic reaction.

Applying these ideas to the Cordillera, geologists suggest that all its mountains were created through the continuing interaction of neighbouring crustal plates. Some of these plates carry the continent of North America, and the others form the ocean floor of the Pacific.

Geologists say that about 400 million years ago North America's continental margin was about 500 km east of where it is now — following a line through the heart of B.C. Wind, water, and frost wore away the granites of the continent, and rivers carried sediment to the sea, where it was laid down on the ocean floor.

These processes of erosion and sedimentation continued for tens of millions of years. Meanwhile, changes in the mantle caused the North American and Pacific plates to collide. Each time they came together, the denser basalt of the Pacific floor plunged beneath the continental plate and melted.

In reaction, molten magma squeezed upwards. In some cases it

British Columbia as seen from space, an effect created through a mosaic of ERTS satellite photographs.

Scores of glaciers flow through the mountains of Glacier National Park, relics of the Ice Age that shaped B.C.'s contours and sculpted its mountains.

penetrated a weak segment of the crust and reached the surface as an arc of volcanoes. More often the crust contained it, but the magma's thrust was so great that it pushed large areas of overlying sediment high above sea level.

That is what happened along B.C.'s present coastline, and in the interior, too. On the coast, volcanic forces have pushed up the sediment on at least three occasions, most recently 100 million years ago. Each time the forces of erosion have sculpted the raised land as a pattern of mountains.

In the interior, the Omineca mountains of the north were not lifted so high and have been less affected by erosion. However, the Columbia mountains of the south-east — the Purcells, Selkirks, and Monashees — and the Cariboos to the north show evidence of nature's devastation.

The effects of erosion are even more dramatic in the Rockies, where ancient

Mineral Deposits

Mountains are often much younger than the rocks that they contain. The Purcell range in the Kootenays of south-eastern B.C. consists of Precambrian sediments among the oldest in Canada and holds deposits of lead and zinc that were already in place 400 million years ago.

In contrast, some base metals were introduced at a late stage, as a result of volcanic activity. Copper and molybdenum are found in the west and in a long belt running through the interior. Lead and zinc are found there, too. In some areas gold is associated with the copper, and silver with the lead and zinc.

There are beds of coal in the Rockies, deposited before the mountains were built. They are accessible in both the south and the north, but as yet only the southern deposits have been exploited. Asbestos is being mined at Cassiar near the Yukon boundary, and oil and natural gas are being extracted from the sediments of the north-eastern plains.

rock was raised up about 50 million years ago, making the Rockies only half as old as the coastal and interior mountains. The range is separated from the interior region by a well-marked depression known as the Rocky mountain trench.

The Rockies are an example of what can happen when plates interlock without forcing each other up or down. The same thing occurred in the Himalayas and in the Appalachians of eastern North America. In each case lateral pressures buckled, folded, and in places tore the sediments' strata and squeezed them upwards, exposing them to the elements.

The west coast of Vancouver Island, originally deep on the ocean floor but thrust above the surface through the movement of the earth's crustal plates.

WOOD AND WATER

British Columbia's mountains face the sea. Like hurdles on a running track, the systems block the path of moist air moving inland from the Pacific and force it upwards. The moisture condenses, causing precipitation.

That is a pattern endlessly repeated on the mountains' western slopes, but on the other side the opposite occurs. The descending air is drained of moisture and thirstily absorbs all the wetness it can find. As a result, the regions beyond each mountain range are exceptionally sunny, at least in the south, and near-desert conditions occur.

These extreme variations are reflected in B.C.'s vegetation patterns, but they are not the only influences. Altitude plays a major role, and the treeline gradually drops from south to north. The sea moderates coastal temperatures and they are quite mild, but farther east there are wide disparities between highs and lows.

Botanists recognize six main vegetation zones in British Columbia. The bleakest is the alpine zone, the highest in which trees survive without being killed by winter blizzards. Stunted black spruce, alpine larch, and limber pine give out at the treeline, but lichens and flowering plants thrive even higher.

The sub-alpine zone covers much of British Columbia at higher levels, both in the interior and nearer the coast. Engelmann spruce, alpine fir, and mountain hemlock are found in most areas, and there are yellow cedar in the west. Trees grow slowly because the soil beneath them thaws for only a short period each summer.

Boreal forest is closely related to the sub-alpine zone and is part of the northern forest belt that stretches right across Canada and on around the world. Its chief features are white and black spruce, balsam fir, jackpine, and aspen. The zone occupies much of northern B.C. and the Peace river country of the north-east.

Montane forest is found in the rain-shadows of the interior plains. It is characterized by open stands of Douglas fir and ponderosa pine, and large areas of sagebrush. The zone also includes grassland, which some botanists treat as a separate vegetation type, even though sagebrush has invaded it in the wake of overgrazing.

B.C.'s coastal forest occurs on both the mainland and the islands. In the south, the Douglas fir is prominent, but farther north it loses ground to the western hemlock and western red cedar. The amabilis fir is found on the mainland and on western Vancouver Island, but does not grow on the Queen Charlotte islands.

The Columbia forest zone is really an interior version of the coastal forest. It includes Douglas fir, western hemlock, western cedar, and also the western larch, which occurs nowhere else. As on the west coast, heavy precipitation means that mosses and lichens flourish, and the forest's interior is dark and damp.

The quiet grandeur of the forests contrasts with the awesome power of

A hiker ascends through sub-alpine forest high above Rogers Pass in Glacier National Park.

B.C.'s rivers. The most famous are the Columbia and the Fraser, which originate in the Rocky mountain trench. At Lytton, the Fraser is joined by the Thompson, which springs from the Cariboo mountains of the interior.

The Skeena river rises in north-central B.C., and reaches the sea near Prince Rupert. Like other rivers emptying into the Pacific, it is famous for its salmon runs. North-eastern rivers, among them the Liard and the Peace, are part of the Mackenzie system and flow eastwards.

There are many outstanding lakes in the province, including Babine, Kootenay, Atlin, Stuart, and those in the Okanagan valley. But the largest is man-made. Williston Lake in the northeast was created by the Bennett Dam, the centrepiece of the Peace river hydroelectric project.

Forests cover roughly 60 per cent of B.C.'s area. They are at their thickest on mountain slopes that catch precipitation, while in contrast some sheltered areas are nearly desert.

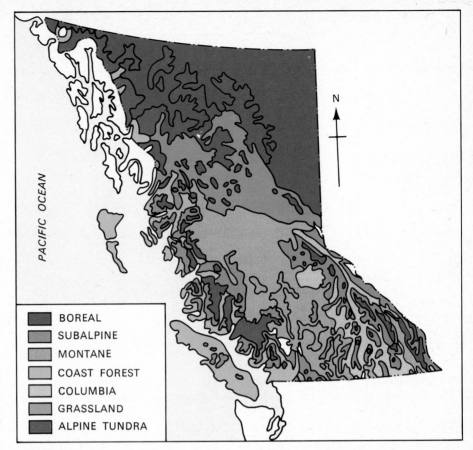

PACIFIC OCEAN

N

- BOREAL
- SUBALPINE
- MONTANE
- COAST FOREST
- COLUMBIA
- GRASSLAND
- ALPINE TUNDRA

Douglas Firs

Known to Indians as the 'real tree,' the Douglas fir is the unchallenged giant of B.C.'s forests. Specimens more than 80 m tall and 600 years old are not uncommon, and there are records of trees twice as old and more than 100 m tall.

The Douglas is not a true fir, but a genus in its own right. It was recognized as such by David Douglas, a Scottish botanist sent to study west coast trees in 1825. The tree can grow in a wide range of soil and climatic conditions, everywhere from the dank rain-forests of the coast to the dry plateaux of the interior.

On the coast, Douglas firs reach greater heights than in the interior, but they are not the climax species. Because they are intolerant of shade, their seedlings spurn the messy conditions of the rain-forest floor and are supplanted by less fastidious species like western hemlock and western red cedar.

The Douglas fir is given a second chance on the coast when there is a fire. Herbaceous plants and alder shrubs help to fix nitrogen in the soil, then Douglas fir and other conifers take root and thrust through the alder cover. Because the Douglas fir grows faster, it can obliterate its competition for centuries at a stretch.

In areas of the interior where Douglas fir grows, the tree cover is not as dense as on the coast. There, adequate sunlight reaches the forest floor, and young Douglas firs are more tolerant of shade and can therefore succeed their parents. Inland, the fir is regarded as the climax species, whereas on the coast it is normally no more than a pioneer.

Dense vegetation clogs the rain forest of the Pacific Rim National Park, on Vancouver Island's west coast.

THE INDIANS

All of North America's Indians lived close to nature, but none more successfully than those of the north Pacific coast. Fat salmon, tall trees, and plentiful furbearers supplied most of their earthly needs, and the beauty of their surroundings sustained their souls.

Abundant food and sympathetic climate attracted large numbers of In- dians to the area. Data for earlier periods is not available, but in 1835 what is now B.C. held one-third of all the Indians in Canada. Two dozen lan- guages were spoken, belonging to seven of Canada's eleven Indian language families.

Most of the Indians lived on the coast or along the western rivers and were markedly different from their in- land cousins. Their lifestyles had much in common with those of ancient peoples in Asia. Anthropologists sup- pose that there was basic kinship be- tween the Indians and Asians, and perhaps continuing contact, too.

The most northerly of British Col- umbia's coastal Indians were the Tsim- shian, really three closely allied groups — the Tsimshian proper on the coast, the Gitksan up the Skeena river, and the Nishga on the Nash river. All three groups hunted salmon, and the Tsimshian pursued sea lions and sea otters.

The Tsimshian bands were notable carvers of totem poles, chests, and masks. They were also accomplished weavers and created spoons and ladles from the horns of mountain goats and mountain sheep. Many of their arts have been resurrected at the model Gitksan village of 'Ksan, on the Skeena river close to Hazelton.

Many of the Tsimshian's beliefs and customs were observed by a more war- like people, the Haida of the Queen Charlotte islands. Like the Tsimshian, the Haida were carvers, not only of red cedar, but of glossy black slate too. Their totem poles were the most refined of all and their canoes were the most elaborate.

The Haida were the most powerful of the coastal tribes. On occasions their expeditions for plunder and slaves car- ried them as far south as Puget Sound, now part of the state of Washington. Some of their ocean-going canoes could carry 60 people. At home, they lived in gabled longhouses fronted by heraldic totem poles.

The Kwakiutl occupied the northern corner of Vancouver Island and the mainland opposite, apart from a small area controlled by the Bella Coolas. Like other coastal tribes, they based their society on the 'potlatch,' a ceremonial feast in which a chief treated his guests to lavish gifts to prove he was worthy of some change in his status.

Guests at a potlatch were expected to reciprocate later, and the demand for gifts provided plenty of work for craftsmen. Besides, woodcarvers made the heraldic crests and totem poles that proclaimed their clan's status. Northern carvers restricted themselves to carving totem poles and masks from a single block of wood, but the Kwakiutl felt free to add beaks and arms and to use bright paint.

The Kwakiutl's territory was almost cut in half by the Bella Coolas, a Salish-speaking group related to the Coastal Salish to the south. The Bella Coolas carved beautiful totem poles and made huge masks with beaks that opened and closed when pulled by concealed ropes.

The areas occupied by B.C.'s Indians in about 1850: 1. Haida; 2. Tsimshian; 3. Kwakiutl; 4. Bella Coola; 5. Nootka; 6. Coastal Salish; 7. Interior Salish; 8. Kootenay; 9. Chilcotin; 10. Carrier; 11. Sekani; 12. Nahani; 13. Kaska; 14. Tahltan; 15. Tlingit.

Inside a lodge in Nootka Sound on Vancouver Island's west coast, 1798. The scene was recorded by John Webber, official artist with Capt. James Cook.

The Coastal Salish, the most numerous of the coastal tribes, did not carve totem poles. Instead, they erected 'welcoming figures' — statues standing up to six metres tall, with both arms raised in salute. Salish women made beautiful baskets and wove blankets from the hair of white dogs bred for the purpose.

The Salish and their flat-roofed longhouses occupied the lower mainland and Vancouver Island's south-east corner. The west coast of Vancouver Island was the home of the Nootka, the only B.C. tribe that preyed on Pacific whales. Specially trained crews would pursue a whale in war canoes, and a harpooner of high rank would stab it to death.

Peoples of the coast and of the islands were relatively settled. Not so the tribes of the interior. They were organized in smaller bands that were frequently on the move in search of better conditions, though most laid claim to traditional hunting and fishing grounds.

The largest of the inland peoples was the Interior Salish, a grouping of five related tribes that spoke different dialects and were frequently at odds with one another. In summer they lived in small cedar lodges that were mere hovels compared with the elegant longhouses on the coast. In winter they dug deep, circular pits and roofed them over.

The Kootenays of south-eastern B.C. were related to the Indians of the plains. They had moved westward over the mountains under pressure from the Blackfoot, probably early in the eighteenth century. Like the plains tribes, they rode horses, lived in teepees painted with animal designs, and dressed entirely in skins and ceremonial bonnets of eagle feathers that were a mark of high honour.

In central and northern B.C. there were a number of Athapaskan-speaking bands. The Chilcotins lived between the Cascade mountains and the Fraser river and were forever at war with the Car-

riers to the north. The Chilcotins traded heavily with coastal Indians, particularly the Bella Coolas.

The Carriers earned their name through an ancient tradition. Carrier widows were expected to bear the charred bones of their husbands on their backs for at least two years. Like the Chilcotins and Interior Salish, many southern Carriers spent the winters in underground lodges, and they, too,

traded extensively with tribes of the coast.

Sekanis lived east of the Carriers, and Tahltan to the north. Both groups struggled for survival and had little opportunity to develop a significant culture. Beavers, Kaskas, and Slaveys, who neighboured them, were people of the woods, and Tlingits to the west were inland relations of the great coastal tribes of Alaska.

Nootka Indians enjoying a feast. An engraving published in Spain in 1802.

The sea otter, the basis of the rich fur trade of the late eighteenth century.

Sea Otters

Atlantic Canada's early fortunes were based on codfish, and Central Canada's on the beaver. On the Pacific coast the chief attraction was the sea otter. Particularly in China, sea otter pelts were regarded as the most beautiful and valuable of all furs.

The sea otter trade began almost by accident, when Russians from the ill-fated Bering expedition of 1741 returned from the Aleutian islands. The survivors had wrapped themselves in sea otter pelts to keep warm, and Chinese traders offered to buy them for high prices. Soon, Russians were visiting the Aleutians to bring back more.

Europeans and Americans entered the sea otter trade when they heard of Capt. Cook's expedition of the 1770s. They acquired pelts from coastal Indians in B.C., then ferried them to China in expectation of huge profits. The trade continued throughout the nineteenth century, and the sea otter came close to extinction.

The last sighting of a 'native' sea otter off Vancouver Island was made in 1929. In 1969 the Canadian and British Columbian governments began introducing animals from the Aleutian islands, and in three years released 89 of them off Vancouver Island. Biologists are sure they are forming colonies again, just as they did in the old days.

NOOTKA SOUND

Juan de Fuca was a Greek navigator in the service of the Spanish. In 1592 he was sent north from Mexico to find a sea passage from the Pacific to the Atlantic. Geographers of the day believed that a 'Strait of Anian' cut through the heart of North America.

For decades, Europeans had been looking for the strait from the Atlantic. Each time their efforts ended in frustration. De Fuca, however, returned with reports of a deep strait opening into a broad gulf. He was convinced that it was the Pacific approach to the fabled north-west passage.

Judging from De Fuca's descriptions, he had discovered the strait between southern Vancouver Island and the mainland, today named in his honour. The find aroused great interest in Europe and particularly in England. Several more expeditions set out to reach the Pacific from the Atlantic, but in the 1770s the British tried a different approach.

This time, an expedition was sent to the Pacific. It consisted of two small ships with Capt. James Cook in overall command. Besides De Fuca's descrip-

Captain James Cook's expedition visits Nootka Sound in 1778. Nootka Indians crowd around the ships to trade furs for whatever metal the British can provide.

tions, Cook was equipped with a fanciful Russian map showing a wide passage between Alaska and land to the south. His main aim was to probe the gap and see where it led.

Cook had intended to investigate De Fuca's strait, but a heavy storm blew his ships out to sea. Instead, in March 1778 he landed at Nootka Sound on the west coast of Vancouver Island. The ships needed repairs before proceeding farther, and Cook went ashore to take advantage of the fine trees growing there.

Local Indians who came out in canoes to investigate the ships were well disposed. In the days that followed they were invited on board, and offered large quantities of furs and curios in exchange for metal of any kind. Cook and his men went ashore and visited Nootka longhouses, and Indians serenaded them wherever they went.

It took four weeks to repair the ships. By that time their holds were full of sea otter pelts and other valuable furs. Cook sailed far to the north, touching land along the way, and penetrated the Bering Strait until stopped by polar ice. For the winter, the ships headed south to the Sandwich islands, today's Hawaii.

There Cook was stabbed to death by islanders. His crews later traded their furs in China for a large profit. Within a few years a number of enterprising merchants were following their example, obtaining furs from the Nootka Indians

and their neighbours and carrying them to the other side of the Pacific.

Most of these merchants were British subjects based in China, and in 1788 several combined to build a fortified post on Nootka Sound. There they were joined by two American traders from Boston, who had reached the Pacific by way of Cape Horn. All these intrusions challenged Spain's trading monopoly in the eastern Pacific.

In 1789 a Spanish man-of-war arrived in Nootka Sound just as the American ships were leaving to sail up the coast. The Spanish regarded the Americans as enemies of the British and therefore let them go, but the British ships were seized and the fort was dismantled. The newcomers built their own fort in its place.

News of the outrage nearly provoked a European war between Britain and Spain, but eventually the Spanish gave way. A British expedition commanded by Capt. George Vancouver was sent to the Pacific to receive the Spanish surrender and to chart the Pacific coast between California and Alaska.

The launching of the *North West America* at Nootka Sound in 1788. The ship was the first to be built in what is now British Columbia.

Vancouver's ships entered the Strait of Juan de Fuca in 1792. After circumnavigating the island that has borne Vancouver's name ever since, they came to Nootka Sound. There the Spanish commandant received Vancouver civilly, but refused to give up more than the site of the old fort.

The issue was confused for some months, until at last the Spanish agreed to restrict themselves to the lands south

Local Indians stand by as Capt. George Vancouver's ship *Discovery* grounds on rocks in Queen Charlotte's Sound in 1793. The ship survived and was floated off at high tide.

of the Columbia river. The coast north of Sitka, in what is now Alaska, already belonged to Russia. Vancouver began a careful exploration of the land between, all of which he claimed for Britain.

11

Alexander Mackenzie, the Scottish-born explorer who reached the Pacific in 1793, making him the first man to cross Canada from sea to sea.

Big Canyon in the Fraser river, as it appeared in the 1860s. The canyon was traversed by Simon Fraser and his men on their journey towards the Pacific.

THE NOR'WESTERS

George Vancouver's exhaustive survey of B.C.'s coastline occupied him for three summers. In June 1793 his boats were at the mouth of the Bella Coola river, barely a month before a young Scottish explorer arrived there after travelling overland from the east.

The explorer was Alexander Mackenzie, a fur trader in the service of the North West Company of Montreal. Mackenzie was the company's chief representative in the Athabasca region, the far north of what is now Alberta. Whether on his own initiative or on instructions, he had set out to find a route to the Pacific.

At the time, the Athabasca region was Canada's north-western frontier, and there was no certain information on what lay west of the Rocky mountains. Mackenzie's first attempt to find out had led him not to the Pacific, but to the Arctic, travelling down the great river which now bears his name.

After spending a year in Britain to learn more of astronomy and navigation, Mackenzie was ready to try again. In May 1793 he set off from Lake Athabasca in a large canoe to paddle up the Peace river. With him were another Scot, six French-speaking voyageur canoemen, and two Indian guides.

The river route up to the mountains tested the skills of the voyageurs to the limit, but was straightforward compared with the challenges they had to meet on the other side. Once across the continental divide they launched the canoe on a swift-flowing stream swollen by melting snow, and lost control of it in rapids.

The canoe hit a rock and ran aground on a gravel bar. The voyageurs refloated it, but the rapids caught it and smashed first the stern and then the bow against more obstructions. The bottom was ripped and the voyageurs were tipped out, but fortunately they clung to the craft until it reached calm water.

Miraculously there were no serious injuries, though much of the cargo was lost. The voyageurs set to work with

molten pitch and patches of oilskin and birchbark, and by nightfall the canoe was watertight again. After a night's rest the party was once more on its way.

The stream led to a small river, and the river led to the main course of a large one — the Fraser. There the explorers met a band of Carrier Indians who told them that the river led south rather than west and was impassable at three points. Besides, there were fierce warriors downstream who would never allow them through.

At this stage Mackenzie and his men were near the site of Alexandria. The Carriers advised them to return upstream to the Blackwater river, by which they could travel towards the west. Then they could cache their canoe and complete the journey to the coast on foot.

Mackenzie followed their advice. The canoe and a supply of food were hidden at the head of the Blackwater. Each man was issued with a heavy pack containing essential supplies, not least trade goods. A Carrier guide was enlisted to lead the party over well-worn trails across the mountains.

The journey to the coast took several days. As the white men approached the sea they noticed a distinct change in climate and vegetation, and saw settlements dominated by towering totem poles. When they arrived in a village of Bella Coolas, they were welcomed with gifts and a feast and were able to borrow a canoe to reach the sea.

So it was that Alexander Mackenzie reached the Pacific, in spite of a last-minute attack by Bella Bella Indians. Beseiged overnight on a bare rock, Mackenzie inscribed a record of his accomplishment in vermilion mixed with grease — *Alex Mackenzie from Canada by land, 22d July 1793.* Fortunately, he and his men escaped the Bella Bellas and returned by the way they had come.

Mackenzie had shown the way across North America, and on his return to Britain he wrote a book about

The routes of the great explorers — George Vancouver, Alexander Mackenzie, Simon Fraser, and David Thompson. Vancouver's men were surveying the mouth of the Bella Coola river barely a month before Mackenzie arrived after travelling overland.

the journey and in 1801 was honoured with a knighthood. His fellow Nor'Westers prepared to profit from his discoveries by taking the fur trade across the mountains and down to the coast.

In 1805 Simon Fraser led a party up the Peace river and across the continental divide, and built Fort McLeod as the first trading post on B.C.'s mainland. In the next year he built two more, Fort St. James and Fort Fraser. Then he set out to find a navigable river route to the sea.

Like Mackenzie, Fraser believed that the tumbling river heading south from the mountains led to the Columbia, and he set out to follow it. The route proved no better than the Carriers had predicted, and soon Fraser and his men had to leave their canoes and follow the banks on foot.

To Fraser's consternation, his river turned westwards and approached the coast far to the north of the Columbia's

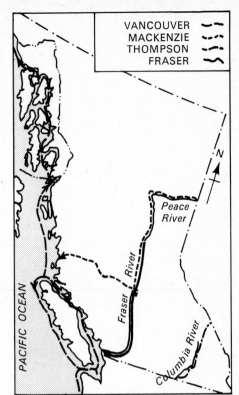

mouth. Disappointed, he was forced to accept that he was on the wrong river and had to retrace his steps. Even so, the river he had explored was to prove one of B.C.'s most important, and ever since it has been known by his name.

B.C.'s rugged terrain forced travellers to make frequent portages in bypassing rapids and falls. A painting by H. J. Warre.

NEW CALEDONIA

Most of the leading Nor'Westers, Mackenzie and Fraser among them, were of Scottish descent. The mountains and even more the lakes west of the Rockies reminded them of Scotland, and they soon named the region 'New Caledonia.'

For some years the Nor'Wester trading posts in New Caledonia were controlled from the Athabasca territory, though the fort on the Columbia was supplied from the sea. Then in 1821 the North West Company was amalgamated with its old rival, the Hudson's Bay Company, and the posts of both were reorganized.

The Hudson's Bay Company sent a veteran Nor'Wester, John McLoughlin, to command its operations on the west coast. McLoughlin reached the Columbia in 1824 and soon noted that coastal Indians were being corrupted. Trading schooners looking for sea otter pelts were supplying the Indians with rum.

To combat the menace, McLoughlin built a new post 70 km up the Columbia and named it Fort Vancouver. The post became his headquarters, and from it he controlled a trading empire that stretched east to the Rockies and south to California. Northwards it reached to Alaska, where Britain and Russia agreed on a border and signed a treaty in 1825.

Each year, brigades several hundred strong travelled in all these regions to hunt and carry supplies to northern trading posts. The brigades bound for New Caledonia travelled by canoe to points south of B.C.'s present border, then transferred their cargo to pack-horses for the journey into the mountains.

Fort Kamloops became the great halfway house for the north-bound brigades, and horses were left there to pasture while fresh animals carried their packs to the interior. The ultimate destination of the northern brigades was Fort St. James north-west of Fort (later Prince) George, high in the mountains and commanded by James Douglas.

The fur trade appeared to be flourishing, but McLoughlin was wor-

B.C. trappers still pursue lynx, beaver, and other creatures of the forest as in the days of New Caledonia. This is a trapper's cabin in the far north of the province.

Fort Victoria on Vancouver Island, as it appeared during the 1840s. Victoria consisted of little more than the fort until overrun by the gold rushes of the 1850s and 1860s.

ried. A constant stream of American immigrants was pouring into the Columbia region in the wake of the Lewis and Clark expedition. In 1838 McLoughlin advised the Hudson's Bay directors to ask for a British garrison that could protect their interests in the west.

The Hudson's Bay Company had weathered many storms before, and the directors were confident they could survive the new one. Expecting the worst, McLoughlin sent James Douglas to choose a site for a trading post on Vancouver Island, which was undisputed British territory.

In 1843 Douglas led a small party to the south of the island, and soon constructed the post later known as Fort Victoria. Around Fort Vancouver the American colonists became increasingly hostile to the company, and in 1844 they established a provisional government of their own.

In 1846 the United States and Britain signed the Oregon Treaty, accepting the 49th parallel as their common border in the west, with a southward kink at the end to accommodate Vancouver Island. Fort Vancouver and the Columbia were surrendered to the Americans, and Fort Victoria became the Pacific headquarters of the British fur trade.

American expansion did not stop with the Oregon Treaty, and by 1848 Hudson's Bay Company officials feared they might lose Vancouver Island and perhaps New Caledonia too. The company asked that the island be made a British colony, and the British parliament agreed.

A London barrister, Richard Blanshard, was sent out as governor. He found that his domain consisted of little more than the trading post and soon returned to Britain in disgust. James Douglas, the Hudson's Bay Company representative, was appointed in his place.

An anonymous painting of a fur trading post in B.C.'s interior, almost certainly Fort Kamloops. The fort was the principal staging post for fur brigades travelling between the Columbia river and the north.

Fort Astoria

The mouth of the Columbia river was discovered by Capt. Robert Gray of Boston in 1792, which meant that the young United States could claim territory on the Pacific. In 1805 the claim was strengthened when an American expedition led by Meriwether Lewis and William Clark reached the river after travelling overland from St. Louis.

Assuming that the Columbia was American, the New York merchant John Jacob Astor established a company to trade furs on the west coast. He recruited a number of experienced traders and voyageurs from the North West Company, and sent some of them to travel overland and some around Cape Horn.

The other Nor'Westers were ready to give Astor a run for his money. Their chief surveyor, David Thompson, travelled west by forced marches and reached the sea in July 1811. Even so, his former colleagues were ahead of him and had already established 'Fort Astoria.'

In 1812 war broke out between the United States and Britain, and Astor prudently sold Fort Astoria to the Nor'Westers. Following the war, both Britain and the United States claimed sovereignty over the region, and in 1818 it was agreed that both nations might trade and establish settlements in the disputed territory.

The road to the Cariboo skirts the Fraser canyon, a remarkable feat of engineering by a military party from Britain. The road project was begun in 1862 and was completed three years later.

Three Cariboo miners pose above their claim on Williams Creek. The timbered shaft was located above gravel that marked the course of an ancient stream.

THE CARIBOO

When gold was discovered in California late in the 1840s, the stream of American migration to the Pacific coast became a flood. As the initial excitement subsided, prospectors spread north to pan streams and rivers for a strike of their own.

Many of the prospectors entered New Caledonia, and some found gold on the Fraser and its tributaries. The miners concerned kept their discoveries to themselves, until in 1858 several of them sailed from Fort Victoria to sell their gold at the mint in San Francisco.

Somehow word leaked out that there was gold on the Fraser, and within two weeks Fort Victoria was inundated by a mob of prospectors clamouring for transportation to the mainland. Victoria's population swelled from a few score to more than 20 000, the majority camped in tents outside the trading post's stockade.

An armada of small vessels carried the fortune-hunters to Fort Langley, a primitive Hudson's Bay outpost on the lower reaches of the Fraser. Thousands more miners entered New Caledonia from the United States. Aged steamers, sailing craft, canoes, wagons, pack-trains, and in many cases their own feet carried them to the goldfields.

The focus of the initial rush was Yale, about 150 km up the Fraser. By the beginning of summer, 10 000 men were in the surrounding area, rocking gravel and washing it for gold. With the best claims already staked, men pressed farther upstream to test gravel beds revealed as the river waters dropped.

In theory, New Caledonia was a land without government. The Hudson's Bay Company had exclusive fur-trading rights, but the British had made no provision for law and order. James Douglas was still governor of Vancouver Island, but his authority did not extend to the mainland.

In practice, the diggers were happy to accept Douglas's word even if it had no official backing. When a serious fight broke out between prospectors and Indians angered by loss of their traditional salmon fishing grounds, Douglas was called in to arbitrate. For good measure he appointed a mining recorder to register claims.

Douglas had barely returned to Victoria when news arrived from Britain. None too soon, the mainland was to be proclaimed a colony. Douglas was to be its governor, and its name was British Columbia. In a brief ceremony at Fort Langley in November 1858, New Caledonia passed out of existence and the new colony was born.

Still prospectors crowded up the Fraser, though as many were leaving the goldfields as were arriving there. Claims were worked out and abandoned, and by 1860 it seemed that the Fraser's days were numbered. Prospectors had spread far up the river and had penetrated the mountains, but spectacular finds were rare.

It was then that four prospectors stumbled on the richest find of all, the valleys of the Cariboo, where there were creekbeds studded with nuggets. In the spring of 1861 there was a rush to the Cariboo that far surpassed the race to the lower Fraser and the region became famous in all quarters of the globe.

Some diggers sluiced their gold from the surface gravel, some probed deeper and dug shafts. Gold was where the prospectors found it, and none could predict where it lay. In many cases latecomers made fortunes, while those

Cariboo miners were quick to harness local streams and rivers, as here on Williams Creek in 1868. Waterwheels could be used to power rock stamps that pulverized quartz containing veins of gold.

who had staked the first claims found they had missed the richest deposits and had wasted their opportunity.

Among the latecomers was Twelve Foot Davis from the Peace river country, who noticed that one of the richest claims was about four metres wider than it should have been and pounced on the margin. Another was Billy Barker, a tenderfoot who staked his claim where gold had no business to be and yet made one of the largest fortunes in the Cariboo.

As the diggers prospered, a town sprang up to cater to their needs, named Barkerville after Billy the tenderfoot. Saloons, stores, hotels, and many other establishments vied for the wealth that the miners produced, and Barkerville's merchants grew rich without having to soil their hands on the diggings.

Unluckily for those not doing so well, Barkerville had the highest prices in North America, because it was far from the coast and transportation services were virtually non-existent. Those travelling in and out had to struggle over makeshift trails or brave the rivers as the explorers had before them.

In 1862 James Douglas set out to improve matters by commissioning military engineers to build a proper highway. The engineers, originally sent out from Britain to survey the boundary with the United States, started work in the Fraser canyon. In some places they blasted a shelf from the rock, in others they constructed massive timber trellises to carry the road across chasms in the canyon wall.

Three more years passed before the highway was complete all the way to Barkerville, and by that time the day of the prospector was done and mining companies were taking over. By any standard the highway was one of the wonders of its age, some 650 km long and traversing some of B.C.'s most difficult terrain.

Some miners dug vertical shafts, some dug horizontally. This is the Neversweat claim on Williams Creek, where Chinese labourers helped the proprietors to tram ore from the working face.

The road to the Cariboo was Douglas's crowning achievement, but by the time it was complete he was no longer governor. There had been complaints from both Vancouver Island and British Columbia that his methods were too autocratic and that he stood in the way of democracy. In the fall of 1864 the British government diplomatically induced him to retire.

Besides undertaking to build a cross-continental railroad, the Dominion government promised British Columbia that it would construct a large dry dock in Esquimalt near Victoria. The dock developed into a naval base that still exists today.

Victoria as it appeared in 1863. The pagoda-like buildings were known as 'the birdcages,' and housed the governments of Vancouver Island and later of the united British Columbia.

CONFEDERATION

Amor de Cosmos was a Nova Scotian who reached Victoria in 1858, in the early days of the gold rush. He soon founded a newspaper, the *British Colonist,* and used its columns to demand responsible government for both the island and the mainland.

The prosperity of the goldfields quickly declined as the best deposits were worked out, and the administrations of the twin colonies found it difficult to raise adequate funds. De Cosmos urged them to unite so that both the island and the mainland could save money, and the enlarged British Columbia came into being in 1866.

At first, New Westminster on the Fraser served as capital, but in 1868 the legislators changed their minds and the whole administration moved over to Victoria. Before that happened, De Cosmos and others were working to persuade British Columbians to join the new Canadian Confederation formed in 1867 by colonies in the east.

In 1868 De Cosmos's 'Confederation League' organized a conference at Yale on the Fraser. There, 26 delegates drew up a set of conditions under which British Columbia might agree to join Canada. One was that Canada should provide a railway link between east and west, and another was that it should absorb the colony's debt.

The Confederation League was supported by many of those living on the mainland, notably the miners of the Cariboo. But it was opposed by two factions. One, composed of civil ser-

Before Vancouver was founded, ships loaded timber in Burrard Inlet from sawmills close to the little settlement of Gastown.

vants and retired Hudson's Bay Company officials, was happy with the status quo. The other, chiefly merchants in Victoria, wanted annexation by the United States.

The merchants went so far as to send a petition to President Ulysses Grant. This so dismayed the majority of colonists that the legislative council discussed Confederation and agreed it might be an advantage. As a result, a delegation of three set off for Ottawa to sound out the Canadians.

The Ottawa negotiations began in June 1870. The delegates had been told to demand responsible government, cancellation of the colony's debt, and new public buildings. In addition, they asked for a coach road from the Red river westward and the start of a western railroad within three years.

To the delegates' delight, Ottawa promised more than they had hoped for. The railroad would be started within two years, not three. A dry dock would be constructed at Esquimalt near Victoria, the finest natural harbour on Vancouver Island, and Ottawa would pressure the British government to maintain a major naval base there.

With promises so grand, British Columbians had no more objections to living in a province like those of the east. So it was that under an imperial order-in-council of 1871, it was declared that 'the said colony of British Columbia shall be admitted into and become part of the Dominion of Canada.'

B.C.'s first provincial election was held in 1871, and John Foster McCreight became the first premier. In its first session, the legislature passed some 90 acts, among them measures ensuring a secret ballot, and the extension of the franchise to all adult males except Indians and Chinese.

Nanaimo's coal deposits made the city B.C.'s most significant industrial centre, one of the major coaling stations on the Pacific coast. This is the fort built by the Hudson's Bay Company, as it appeared in 1859.

Sea to Sea

When British Columbia's delegates travelled to Ottawa in 1870, it was possible to cross the continent by rail, but by a roundabout route. First the delegates had to sail to San Francisco, then catch a train to Sacramento.

From Sacramento, they entrained for Chicago, but would have had to change trains several times on the way. From Chicago, railroads led to Detroit and then to Buffalo, and so to Toronto and ultimately Ottawa. Such a journey took more than two weeks, but it was the quickest route available.

San Francisco's rail connections gave it great advantages over the little towns in B.C., and made them dependent on supplies shipped from the United States. Besides, San Francisco now served countries all around the Pacific rim — a trade that B.C. could share in if a railroad connected the colony with ports on the Atlantic.

One of the first men to advocate such a railroad was Alfred Waddington, the inspector of schools on Vancouver Island. During the 1860s Waddington used his own resources to develop an ill-fated coach road to the interior, and then began lobbying for a railroad. On his tombstone he is described as 'Founder of the CPR.'

Public Archives Canada, C-9561

19

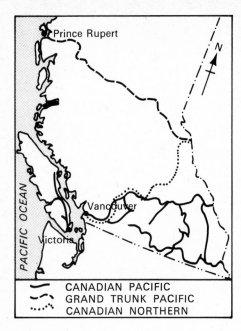

The routes chosen by B.C.'s pioneer railroads.

The mountains and gorges of B.C. posed considerable challenges for the CPR's engineers. Fortunately there was no shortage of timber to build trellis bridges.

THE RAILROADS

As part of its agreement with British Columbia, the Canadian government prepared to build its railroad across the continent. A Scotsman, Sandford Fleming, was appointed engineer-in-chief, and survey crews were sent to search out the best route through the Rockies.

Early in 1872, the Canadian government announced two important decisions. The first was that the railroad would be routed through the Yellowhead Pass. The second was that it would be built and operated by private enterprise, though the undertaking would be subsidized by the government.

Almost immediately, rival consortiums of railroad builders were formed in Toronto and Montreal. Under pressure from the government and particularly the prime minister, Sir John A. Macdonald, the two agreed to unite as the Canadian Pacific Railway, headed by Sir Hugh Allan of Montreal.

It soon came to light that Sir Hugh had contributed to Conservative party funds in the previous election. Macdonald's government resigned under the cloud of the 'Pacific Scandal.' In the election of 1873 the Conservatives were defeated by the Liberals led by Alexander Mackenzie (no relation to the explorer).

The Liberals did their best to persuade British Columbians to accept much less than the Conservatives had promised, at least until more funds were available. As a stopgap they offered a wagon road, a telegraph line, and a railroad from Esquimalt to Nanaimo on Vancouver Island — a distance of about 70 km.

British Columbians were becoming increasingly frustrated by the delay, and there was dark talk of separation from Canada. In the event, Macdonald and his Conservatives were returned to power in 1878, and impetus was restored. The Canadian Pacific Railway prepared to begin construction.

In the east, the railway was taking over several lines already built by the government. It planned to connect them

National Photography Collection, PA-66576

20

The famous photograph taken as Donald Smith, later Lord Strathcona, drove home the last spike of the Canadian Pacific Railway. It happened at Craigellachie in November 1885.

and extend them west towards the Rockies. At the same time the company was starting construction across the mountain barrier, aiming not for the Yellowhead Pass but instead for Kicking Horse.

The route was changed because the Conservatives feared American expansion to the south. With a railroad passing close to the 49th parallel, troops could be railed in to defend the border. For B.C., the change meant that the railway would reach the sea near New Westminster rather than far to the north.

Construction was scheduled to take place over many years. In the west, it began at Yale in May 1880. An American engineer, Andrew Onderdonk, was contracted to build a line through the Fraser and Thompson canyons, as far as Savona. Later, he was asked to extend it to the Monashees, to meet the line approaching from the east.

Fifteen tunnels had to be built along the first section of the route, and a large army of construction workers was required. When he ran short of men, Onderdonk began importing labourers from China — to the dismay of those who wanted to keep B.C. white. Many years passed before the Chinese were given rights of citizenship.

Onderdonk laboured for five years on his section of the railroad. Meanwhile, eastern crews laid the track across the Rockies and then the Selkirks by way of a pass discovered by Major A.B. Rogers in 1881. In November 1885 Donald A. Smith, one of the railroad's leading financiers, drove the last spike at Craigellachie in Eagle Pass.

At first the CPR line extended only to Port Moody at the head of Burrard Inlet. Sea-going ships could reach the spot, but it could never become a major harbour. The railroad was quickly extended 10 km westwards to the village of Granville, which the CPR renamed

The whole town turns out as the first train reaches Prince Rupert in 1914. The town was especially constructed as the terminus of a transcontinental railroad to rival the CPR.

Vancouver in spite of confusion with the island.

For years the CPR remained Canada's only transcontinental railroad. Gradually Western Canada filled with settlers, who produced so much business that the CPR could not cope with it all. At the turn of the century the Liberal government in Ottawa sanctioned not one but two new lines.

Both the newcomers were to be routed through the Yellowhead Pass. One was the Canadian Northern, heading for Vancouver. The other was the Grand Trunk Pacific, which was to reach the sea at the mouth of the Skeena river in the north — the site of Prince Rupert.

Construction of Prince Rupert began in 1908, and crews started work on the railroad. Like the CPR men, they faced immense challenges in blasting cuts and tunnels through the rugged mountains of the interior. Western and eastern construction crews met at Finmore in 1914, nearly 600 km from the coast.

The Canadian Northern was completed in the following year. Unfortunately for the new railroads, Canada was in the grip of depression. The Grand Trunk Pacific lost money from the start, and was soon taken over by the Dominion government. The Canadian Northern did better, but in 1923 it too became part of the government-owned Canadian National Railways.

PACIFIC RIM

British Columbians demanded the transcontinental railroad, but in sanctioning it, Canada's government was looking far beyond the west coast. In 1879 the federal minister of railways, Charles Tupper, moved an important resolution in the House of Commons.

The resolution stated: 'That the Pacific Railway will form an Imperial Highway across the Continent of

Japanese Canadians removed from their homes on the coast during World War II greet friends and relatives transported to B.C.'s interior ahead of them.

America entirely on British soil, and would form a new and important route from England to Australia, to India and to all the dependencies of Great Britain, as also China and Japan.'

Nearly all these countries were located on the Pacific rim, sharing it with Russia, Latin America, the United States, and British Columbia. All represented major trading opportunities, and the CPR promised that its line would not be complete until there were ocean connections with the ports of the orient.

As a first step, sailing ships arrived at Port Moody in 1886 carrying tea from Japan. In the next year three old Cunard liners began a passenger and mail service between Vancouver and Yokohama, and in 1889 this was extended to reach Shanghai and Hong

The *S.S. Empress of India,* **part of the fleet of passenger and cargo ships that linked Canada with the Far East, visits Vancouver in the early 1900s.**

Kong on the China coast.

Vancouver was closer to the orient than its chief rival, San Francisco, but the American port was closer to Australia. Not until the 1890s were there regular sailings between Vancouver and the antipodes, but they were soon reinforced when an undersea telegraph cable was laid across the Pacific. Linking Vancouver Island with Australia, it was ready for use in 1902.

B.C.'s ties with the western United States had been strong for generations. In 1914 the Panama Canal was opened, and the province was given an easy shipping route to eastern North America and Europe. In the same year half the world went to war, and there were repercussions in the Pacific as German raiders threatened allied shipping.

During World War I Japan was a valued ally, but the position was very different in World War II. Late in 1941 the Japanese entered the war by simultaneously attacking Hong Kong, Thailand, Singapore, and Hawaii. Before long they occupied islands in the Aleutian chain, and seemed poised to invade Alaska.

At the time, there was no efficient overland trail linking Alaska with the rest of the continent. Canada agreed to allow the United States to build a makeshift highway through northern B.C. and the Yukon. Based at Dawson Creek and Whitehorse, the Americans began work in mid-1942 and completed the road within seven months.

To protect B.C., Canada took a step that is now regretted. Many thousands of Canadians with Japanese ancestry were living on the coast, the result of a steady wave of immigration that began in the 1890s. Factions in B.C. feared that the Japanese Canadians might collaborate with the enemy, and pressured the federal government into relocating them where they could do no harm.

In all, 21 000 Japanese Canadians were forcibly moved to B.C.'s interior, Alberta, or Ontario. Their property was seized and auctioned off, and after the war it was suggested they should be deported. Fortunately for Canada, that decision was reversed in 1947 and Japanese Canadians now play prominent roles in all walks of life.

National Photography Collection, PA-11629

Mounted on springboards (with a dog), loggers use axes to notch a Douglas fir before attacking it with a two-handed crosscut saw.

The Loggers

The great trees of British Columbia were only waiting to be felled. The goldseekers and then the railroad builders had needed large quantities of lumber, and there were markets all around the Pacific rim. From an early stage the woods echoed with the thud of axes and the rasp of saws.

To fall a tree, loggers cut notches in the trunk to hold springboard platforms. Standing on the springboards, they cut a deep gash on one side of the trunk to control the tree's lean. Then they sawed through from the other side, pushing and pulling the long crosscut saw until the wood toppled.

The loggers relied on rivers to carry logs to sawmills or to the coast for loading on to ships. They first cut trees close to watercourses, manhandling them with levers and peavies — long poles with a spike on the end. Then they introduced teams of oxen and horses to drag the trees down log skidways.

As logging moved farther from the water, loggers used steam 'donkeys' to haul fallen timber by cable. The system was known as 'ground lead,' because both ends of the log trailed the ground. To avoid obstacles, loggers rigged pulleys on tall spars and dragged logs by 'high lead,' with the front end up in the air.

In the early 1900s logging railways were introduced, and in the 1920s the first logging trucks appeared. By that time British Columbia's forest industries had diversified. There were pulpmills and plywood producers as well as sawmills, and many thousands of men were employed in the forests and in the mills.

Before 1914, most of B.C.'s forest products were railed eastward or shipped to the western United States. Then the Panama Canal was opened. British Columbians found it profitable to ship their products all the way to Europe, and their forest industries expanded rapidly.

THE ECONOMY

Like the rest of North America, British Columbia was hit hard by the Depression of the 1930s. Industries faltered, jobs were scarce, and unemployed men arriving from elsewhere in Canada were housed in workcamps to keep them out of mischief.

World War II revived B.C.'s prosperity. Lumber, base metals, and agricultural produce were needed for the war effort. Ships and aircraft were built in Vancouver and more ships in Victoria. New factories were opened, and both men and women from other parts of Canada arrived in search of work.

A fleet of ferries keeps B.C.'s many offshore islands in contact with the mainland and with one another.

Social Credit

The early 1950s saw a momentous change of government in British Columbia. Since 1941 the province had been governed by a coalition of Liberals and Conservatives, originally formed to thwart a bid for power by the socialist Co-operative Commonwealth Federation.

By 1952 the coalition was breaking apart, and the two parties separated to fight a provincial election. They were beaten by both the CCF and a new party, the Social Credit League. Much of the new party's impetus came from Alberta, but it was led by a disenchanted former Conservative, W.A.C. Bennett of Kelowna.

As first formulated, Social Credit had been an attempt to boost consumer spending by issuing dividends to the public. By the 1950s the movement was committed to defending private enterprise in all its forms, and to adopting good ideas from wherever they could be found. That was to be the pattern of Social Credit in B.C.

W.A.C. Bennett was asked to form a government, and in the next year he called an election. His party gained a majority and set to work to build new highways in the interior. Bennett held on to power until 1972, when the Social Crediters were defeated by the New Democratic Party. Bennett's son Bill took his father's place, and led the Social Crediters back into office in 1975.

W.A.C. Bennett became premier of B.C. in 1952 and held on to power until 1974.

The moderate prosperity continued after the war, but B.C.'s population was still small and was concentrated around Vancouver and Victoria. The interior and the north were virtually empty, until in the late 1940s natural gas was discovered near Dawson Creek, far away in the Peace river country.

The gas field was an extension of those already discovered in Alberta. So was B.C.'s first oilfield, found near Fort St. John in 1952. The north-east swarmed with prospectors and survey teams looking for new sources of petroleum, and pipelines were built to carry fuel to Vancouver.

For B.C., the 1950s were a period of preparation for the future. It was clear that the interior held vast quantities of low-grade base metals and forest resources too, but there was much to be done before they could be exploited. Markets had to be opened, money raised, and transport systems improved.

All that was accomplished, and in the 1960s B.C. surged ahead. Pulp and lumber mills came into production all over the province, and vast new open-pit copper and molybdenum mines were brought on stream. The whole economy boomed and the population expanded rapidly.

That trend continues today, for B.C. still relies heavily on its natural resources. Forest products—chiefly lumber, newsprint, pulp, and plywood—generate nearly 50 cents of each dollar earned. They are sold on four continents, and so are B.C.'s base metals. Most of its coal goes to Japan.

In the past, many of B.C.'s resources were exported with little or no value added through processing. That is no longer the case. Pulpmills, lumber mills, smelters, and refineries are among the province's largest employers. In many areas of the north and the interior they are the chief element of the local economy.

Fish and agricultural processing is less profitable than forestry and mining, but it makes important contributions. Most fish processors are located in the lower mainland and around Prince Rupert, but fishermen are active all along the coast and off the islands, too.

B.C.'s farms crowd not only the lower mainland and southern Vancouver Island, but also special districts like the Okanagan valley and the Peace river country beyond the mountains. Vegetables, grain, beef, dairy products, and poultry help to feed the province, and there is a major export market for apples and other tree fruits.

As yet, most manufacturing activity is based in the lower mainland, within easy reach of nearly 70 per cent of the

Mining is B.C.'s second largest industry, based chiefly on extensive deposits of copper and other base metals in the interior. This is a load-haul-dumper in the Craigmont copper mine.

population. However, cities of the interior are developing too. There are new industries all over the south and in the north as well.

In the mountains, much of this development must take place in two well-defined corridors that together form a T. One corridor, the stem of the T, extends from Hope to Prince George. The other, the bar of the T, follows the Yellowhead Highway that stretches from Prince Rupert to Prince George and beyond towards Edmonton, Alberta.

Environmental considerations take first priority, but several of the powerful rivers that frustrated the explorers have been harnessed to produce electricity. The Kootenay, Columbia, Peace, and several smaller rivers are being used, but many of the best sites have been left alone because dams would disrupt salmon runs.

B.C.'s 'super natural' grandeur is the stock-in-trade of its quickest-growing industry, tourism. Vancouver and Victoria are the chief attractions for out-of-province visitors, but there are five national parks and more than 300 provincial parks to tempt them farther afield.

AGRICULTURE

Less than three per cent of British Columbia's land area is suitable for agriculture. Even so, there are 19 000 farms in the province, and agriculture is the fourth most valuable industry after forestry, mining, and tourism.

Four main regions are involved. In the lower mainland and in southern Vancouver Island, farms concentrate on dairy cattle, poultry, small fruits, and field crops. Those in the valleys of the southern interior specialize in tree fruits. The central interior is ranching country, and the Peace river district raises grain.

As far back as the early 1800s, fur traders started small farms to supply themselves with fresh produce. From the 1820s they also maintained large ranches at Forts Kamloops and Alexandria. There they bred horses and mules for the north country brigades and grew forage crops to feed them.

Cattle were driven to the Cariboo from the United States to supply the gold diggers, and that was the start of the beef industry. Grain and other crops

were raised in the Cariboo and on Vancouver Island. By the 1870s there were 11 grist mills in B.C., supplying flour to the local market.

The first settlers in the Okanagan valley raised cattle and grain, but from the 1890s many grew fruit instead, ferrying their produce to market by shallow-draft sternwheelers. Meanwhile, the Fraser valley was being farmed to supply the growing city of Vancouver, and the Peace river country was opened up by homesteaders.

Today, dairying is the greatest single source of B.C.'s agricultural income. The Fraser valley produces nearly 90 per cent of all the milk, most of it destined for the Vancouver area. The average dairy herd contains more than 60 cows, and black and white Holsteins are the favourite breed.

B.C.'s biggest ranches are in the Kamloops region and the Cariboo, but cattle are also raised in the Kootenays and the Peace river area. At present, half of the calves produced are shipped out of the province before their first winter, because there is not enough feed.

Special feed for Holstein dairy cattle at a farm in the Fraser valley, the region which produces 90 per cent of B.C.'s milk supply.

There are plans to open new areas for summer grazing, which will allow farmers to grow forage crops on land now used as pasture. The extra forage will be used to feed more cattle during winter, the cattle will be slaughtered locally, and there will be no need to import so much beef from outside the province.

Flocks of sheep and goats are raised in the central interior, but most poultry and swine farms are in the Fraser and Okanagan valleys and on Vancouver Island. Poultry farms specialize in eggs, chicken meat, or turkeys, and use factory techniques to maintain a constant supply.

The most valuable crops grown in B.C. are the tree fruits of the interior valleys, particularly the Okanagan, Similkameen, and Kootenay. Once fit only for grazing cattle, the valleys have been transformed by irrigation and now

B.C. grows one-third of all Canada's apples, and produces a valuable surplus for export. Most are produced in the Okanagan valley.

produce one-third of all the fruit grown in Canada.

Apples are the most valuable segment of the tree fruit crop, and amount to one-third of Canada's total output. The valleys also produce all Canada's apricots, half the pears and prunes, 60 per cent of the sweet cherries, and 20 per cent of the peaches.

The Okanagan valley is also famous for its grapes. Most vineyards are located between Kelowna and Osoyoos, and they grow 20 commercial grape varieties. About 90 per cent of the crop goes to local wineries, where it is blended with wines imported from California.

The Fraser valley is one of the world's top producers of raspberries, and its crop amounts to about 95 per cent of Canada's total. Strawberries do well on the coast, and blueberries and cranberries are grown in peat soil near Vancouver. Blueberries and loganberries are a specialty of Vancouver Island.

Vegetables are raised in many parts of the province, but the Fraser valley grows most. Market gardeners produce onions, cabbages, lettuce, and other varieties for the fresh market, but some are grown for processors. The interior valleys are warm enough to support heat-loving vegetables like asparagus, cucumber, peppers, and tomatoes.

The long summer days and flat terrain of the Peace river country make it B.C.'s chief grain producer. Barley is the dominant crop, followed by rapeseed, wheat, forage crops, and fine seeds. The Kootenays produce a lesser volume of cereals and forage, useful to cattle ranchers.

The proportion will increase, but B.C. now meets about 45 per cent of its food needs. It is self-sufficient in dairy and poultry products and vegetables, and fruit is exported. To protect local farmers from competition, most products are regulated by national or provincial marketing boards.

The Okanagan valley is famous for its grapes, most of which are crushed to make British Columbia's wine.

FIBRE FARMERS

A farmer sows seed and harvests his crop within a few months. A forester plants a tree but will probably not live to see it full grown. In spite of the different time scale, modern forest management is really a type of farming.

For both farmer and forester, the cycle of their program begins with the harvest. In the forest, logging crews 'clearcut' all the trees in a stand that may be several hectares in extent. Only stumps and 'slash' remain, and the soil is available for an entirely new growth.

The clearcut stand is gone, but all around are mature trees that will help to reseed it. To give the seeds a chance, the slash remaining after logging is burned, or bulldozers may drag heavy, spiked chains over the whole area. This

Nursery workers on Vancouver Island thin seedlings that will eventually be transplanted to a forest stand.

The Enemies

Fire, insect pests, and disease are the three main challenges to the healthy forest. Each is a tool of nature that disposes of the old to make way for the new, but the forest manager prefers to do the same job in his own time.

Fire is the most spectacular of these challenges. Down the centuries wildfires set off by lightning have destroyed millions of hectares of forest all over the province. Even today, lightning is responsible for over one-third of B.C.'s fires, but most of the rest are caused by human carelessness.

In the fire season, lookouts in towers and spotter aircraft watch over the vulnerable regions. When they notice smoke, an army of firefighters is mobilized by radio. Air tankers, helicopters, and ground crews are rushed to the scene, and race to contain the fire before it can spread.

Fire protection has become so efficient that nearly all outbreaks can be controlled within 24 hours of detection. Today, less wood is lost to fire than to insects and disease, which have been recognized as the major problems in B.C. The forester must contend not only with native pests, but with a number brought in from outside.

Bark beetles worm inside the trees, out of reach of insecticides. Spruce budworm, tussock moths, and other defoliators feast on conifer needles, while forest tent caterpillars and gypsy moths feast on deciduous species. Heart rot or root rot attack the wood from within, and rust kills both cones and needles.

In some cases stands of trees can be saved by the use of chemical insecticides, or by baiting a trap-tree with sexual attractants and then killing the insects that gather there. But in many cases there is no cure, and the only answer is to log the affected stand and prevent the epidemic from spreading.

Forest fires used to be a major menace, but fire-fighting has become so efficient that most outbreaks can be brought under control soon after detection.

process, known as scarifying, mixes the slash and soil and leaves bare earth in which the seeds can take root.

In some areas natural regeneration is sufficient. In others, the forester wants to speed up the process. Tree-planting crews in extended line tramp over the stand carrying bags of seedlings, digging holes with mattocks or dibbles and planting trees at predetermined intervals among the stumps until the whole area is covered.

Most of the seedlings are the progeny of outstanding parents — tall, straight, well-formed, and healthy. Foresters identify these special trees and collect their cones. Then their seeds are raised at one of B.C.'s forest nurseries, whether in greenhouse conditions (for one year) or out of doors (for two).

Each year, the nurseries raise more than 75 million seedlings, which are then transplanted to areas needing reforestation. About 50 per cent of the young stock is Douglas fir destined for the coast. Another 20 per cent is spruce for the interior, 13 per cent is lodgepole pine, and most of the remainder is Sitka spruce, hemlock, or cedar.

Other species will mature more quickly, but Douglas firs need 50 to 80 years growth before they are ready for harvesting. In the interval, foresters protect them against fire, insect pests, and disease. Besides, it may be helpful to thin the growing stand and provide the strongest trees with room to expand.

While the forest is growing, it can serve many purposes. The young stand makes prime wildlife habitat, whether for birds or mammals. It may also have recreational potential, particularly as the access roads built by logging companies are normally open to the public and the government and forest companies maintain special campsites in the woods.

Even more important, the forest produces oxygen — the clean air that makes B.C. such a fine place to live. Besides, the trees check water run-off from the mountains, meaning that streams and rivers are protected from

excessive silt. When a neighbouring area is logged or destroyed by fire, seeds from the trees help to regenerate it.

Meanwhile, the trees grow. At regular intervals the B.C. government compiles an inventory of all that the forest contains. When it knows how much wood the forest is producing, it can decide how much of it the logging companies may harvest. That way the forest's yield is sustained, and its fibre can be farmed forever.

With mattocks and a bag of seedlings, a line of tree-planters advances over a logged-out area and helps the forest to re-establish itself.

FOREST PRODUCTS

Long-term plans are submitted and approved, forest access roads are cut, and loggers and their equipment arrive in the area to be harvested. The loggers have a clear idea of each tree's potential, and aim to extract the maximum value with minimum waste.

In some parts of the interior, trees are removed wholesale and are sent for pulping. Elsewhere, more care must be used. Young trees that can be used as poles or pilings are logged first. Then the loggers attend to larger trees that have potential as lumber or plywood or as pulpwood if they are defective.

Fallers cut the trees and buckers trim them to sizes that the mills can handle. Then heavy machines — mobile spars in Douglas fir country — move the logs to the roadside. Trucks carry them to a sorting area, whether on dry land or in water where they are manoeuvred by miniature tugs known as dozers or boom scooters.

The logs are sorted according to size and species, and as required, they are transported to the mill. In the interior they may be loaded on to trucks or rail flatcars, or formed into raft-like booms and floated on rivers and lakes. On the coast, most mills are located on tidewater so that logs are moved by sea.

In calm conditions, logs can reach the mill in a boom towed by a tug. Across open water — for instance, between the Queen Charlottes and the mainland — they are carried on self-dumping barges. At the mill a barge's ballast tanks are flooded on one side so that it gently tips and dumps its cargo in the water.

In the past, mills operated independently and there was considerable waste. Now it is common for two types of mill to work together — for example, when a plywood mill delivers its reject material to a lumber mill, or when wood chips and sawdust produced by a lumber mill become the raw material of a pulp and paper complex.

Quite different techniques are used at the various mills, even when they are in the same branch of the industry.

A logger scrambles clear as a mighty Douglas fir topples to earth. Behind it are the trunks of trees already fallen.

However, the great majority of them (more than 2000 establishments, large and small) produce lumber, while there are only 30 plywood mills and even fewer pulp and paper mills.

More than half of the lumber comes from the interior region, and most of it is exported to the United States for use in light construction. Larger trees on the coast provide the more valuable 'clear' lumber, noted for its beauty, strength, and durability and also important in the construction industry.

Depending on its markets, a sawmill can produce boards in many sizes. A head-rig saw cuts parallel faces on each log, then a set of gang saws divides it into boards. An edger removes sloping sides, and trim saws square the ends. Each board is classified, then cured to reduce its moisture content.

At a plywood mill, each log is debarked by friction, then mounted on a lathe. As the log spins, a steel blade peels off a thin veneer that is trimmed into various widths. The veneer sheets are dried and sorted according to quality — face pieces, cross bands, and core ply.

When ready, the veneers are assembled at a glue table. Face pieces form

Sawmills large and small are found throughout B.C., both on the coast and in the interior. This one is close to Revelstoke.

the outsides of the plywood panel, while core ply makes up the centre. Cross bands are made up of random widths laid across the grain between the faces and the core. The layers are glued together and bonded in a hot press.

To make woodpulp, the various pulp and paper mills employ three main processes. Two of them are chemical, a matter of cooking wood chips to break down the lignin that binds the fibres together. The third is mechanical, holding logs against a revolving grindstone. B.C. wood fibres are longer than most, and are used to make high grades of

A self-tipping barge carrying wood from the Queen Charlotte islands is towed into Howe Sound on the mainland. With water pumped into its tanks, the barge lists to one side and its cargo slips into the water.

paper and other products.

There are lumber, plywood, and pulp and paper producers all through the interior, but the heaviest concentration is in the lower mainland and on Vancouver Island. Those areas also hold a number of specialist mills that produce construction shingles (tapered) and shakes (straight) from the wood of the western red cedar.

BASE METALS

Before the 1880s, the thousands of miners who converged on British Columbia were interested only in gold. Gradually the placer deposits of alluvial gold were worked out, and companies were formed to mine lode deposits found in hard rock.

The mining companies recovered both gold and silver, the precious metals they were seeking, and at the same time located deposits of base metals like lead, zinc, and copper. From the 1890s copper was mined as a by-product of gold

and silver, and ultimately it was exploited for its own sake.

The early copper mines were underground operations and relatively small-scale. Then in the 1950s a syndicate was formed to mine a large low-grade deposit in the Highland valley southwest of Kamloops. That was the start of the Bethlehem mine, which went into production in 1962 and is still recovering ore from its open pits.

B.C. now has several more major surface mines, among them the Lornex mine in Highland Valley, which is the largest copper producer in Canada.

The Endako molybdenum mine in B.C.'s interior. To prevent cave-ins, the mine is worked as a series of concentric 'benches.'

Apart from one operation on Vancouver Island, the others are in the heart of the Cordillera. All are copper producers, but at the Endako mine the principal mineral is molybdenum.

Open-pit mines use heavy earthmoving equipment to shift ore and waste rock from a giant's stairway of benches that reduce the risk of cave-ins. The benches are drilled and blasted in sequence, and the pit is steadily enlarged as broken rock is trucked to the surface plant to be crushed and concentrated for smelting.

Prices fluctuate, but copper usually contributes half the value of metal produced in B.C. The ore is concentrated at the mines to dispose of surplus weight, then exported to other countries where it is smelted and refined. Only a small proportion is smelted locally. Molybdenum is the second most valuable base metal, much of it a by-product of copper operations.

Before the 1960s, copper and molybdenum were much less important than lead and zinc. These metals often occur together, often accompanied by

A jumbo rig at Craigmont copper mine drills several holes simultaneously, ready for explosives that will tear copper-bearing ore from the working face.

Huge mills containing steel rods or balls grind ore into fine particles that can be processed as copper concentrate, as in this plant at Gibraltar copper mine in B.C.'s interior.

other minerals that can be recovered at the same time. Most of B.C.'s production comes from the Kootenays of the south-east — in fact, from a single source, the Sullivan mine in Kimberley.

The Sullivan was discovered in 1892, a mountain of base metals that was to prove the largest lead-zinc mine in the world. A town that developed near by was named Kimberley after the diamond city in South Africa. The CPR introduced a rail line, and ore from the Sullivan was shipped to a smelter in Trail.

At first, only lead was produced because of difficulties in separating zinc and other metals from the sulphur in the ore. Not until 1920 was there a satisfactory method, and by then both the mine and the smelter had been acquired by the CPR. Soon zinc became the Sullivan's most valuable metal.

Mining methods at the Sullivan have changed with the times. In the early days the accent was on manual labour. Today, heavy machines have quintupled productivity and have revolutionized processes in the surface plant. Lead and zinc concentrates are processed in separate smelters, and by-products include silver, bismuth, cadmium, indium, gold, and antimony.

Smelting and Refining

Most of B.C.'s copper and molybdenum output is exported as concentrate, but some metals are processed locally. Lead and zinc are smelted and refined at Trail, copper is smelted near Kamloops, and aluminum is produced at Kitimat near Prince Rupert.

There has been smelting at Trail since 1895, when a smelter was built to process gold and copper from the Rossland field near by. In 1898 the smelter was sold to the CPR, which soon acquired several local mines. However, Trail did not become important until 1920, when new methods were used to treat lead and zinc from Kimberley.

Today, the Trail smelting and refining complex is one of the world's largest. Finely ground lead and zinc concentrates are railed in from several sources, among them the Pine Point mine in the Northwest Territories. Smelting burns off sulphur dioxide and other impurities. Then the metals are refined electrolytically (though by different methods), remelted, and cast for export.

Trail produces finished pigs of lead and slabs of zinc, but the new Afton smelter near Kamloops stops short of refining copper from the nearby mine. Instead, copper concentrate is charged to the blast furnaces, slag is floated off, and the molten copper is cast as 'blister' billets that are exported for refining elsewhere.

Both Trail and Afton treat local ores, but the aluminum smelter at Kitimat imports most of its raw material from Australia. Kitimat's justification is the ready availability of electricity, the key to the aluminum smelting process. Powder-like alumina is dissolved in molten cryolite, and a heavy electrical charge decomposes it as oxygen and pure aluminum.

The aluminum smelter at Kitimat on B.C.'s north coast, where local electricity is used to process alumina shipped from Australia and other sources.

FOSSIL FUELS

Until 1883, gold was the most valuable mineral produced in B.C. Then it was overtaken, not by base metals, but by coal. Nearly all the coal was mined on the east coast of Vancouver Island.

Coal had been discovered near Port Hardy at the island's northern tip in 1835, and the Hudson's Bay Company had imported 50 miners from Scotland to work it. In 1849, much larger deposits were found at Nanaimo, just in time for the gold rush. The company brought more miners from Britain, and the new pits were soon in production.

Some of the coal was supplied to steamships, some was used for domestic heating, and much of it was exported to California. In 1888 yet more mines were opened at Comox, north of Nanaimo. At the same time, prospectors were examining large deposits of coal in the Crowsnest Pass through the Kootenays that spanned the Alberta boundary.

In 1898 the CPR built a railroad through the pass to reach the coal, and Crowsnest was in business. By 1910 there were mines at Fernie and several other locations, all worked underground. Some of the coal was supplied to the CPR, some was roasted as coke for use in the smelters at Trail and elsewhere.

The coal industry thrived until about 1950, when there was a disastrous slump. Cheap oil and natural gas were available, and many industrial plants switched from coal to other fuels. The domestic heating market declined for the same reason. Most serious of all, the railroads switched from steam locomotion to diesel.

The industry was at a low ebb for nearly two decades. Nanaimo's production ceased altogether, and several Crowsnest mines closed too. Then a new market opened in the late 1960s. The Japanese steel industry needed coking coal, and several Canadian companies signed long-term contracts to

Industrial Minerals

Apart from the Wesfrob iron ore mine in the Queen Charlotte islands, B.C.'s most remote mining operation is at Cassiar, barely 70 km from the Yukon boundary. Cassiar produces chrysotile asbestos, and is the only such mine in the province.

The Cassiar deposits were first recognized in 1950. For many years all production was trucked to Whitehorse in the Yukon and railed over the mountains to Skagway in Alaska. Then a road was built from Cassiar to Stewart, on the border of the Alaska Panhandle. Now the asbestos is trucked south and shipped from within the province.

Much of Cassiar's asbestos is exported, but other industrial minerals are consumed locally. Stone, sand, shale, and clay are drawn from many sources. Gypsum comes from Windermere. Limestone is produced on Texada Island in Georgia Strait, opposite Courtenay, and rock fill is quarried near Vancouver.

Sulphur to make sulphuric acid comes from smelter gases at Trail, and from 'scrubbing' natural gas at Taylor. Nephrite jade, much in demand as a gemstone, is being mined at Ogden Mountain in north-central B.C. and exported to a number of countries including Taiwan.

Cheerful roughnecks at work on a drilling rig near Fort St. John in northern B.C. Both oil and natural gas are being exploited.

Coal loading operations at the Sparwood surface coal mine in B.C.'s Kootenays.

export large quantities.

Today, coking coal from the Kootenays is sold to customers as far away as Brazil, South Korea, and Rumania. Thermal coal, less valuable than the metallurgical variety, is being shipped to Ontario on an experimental basis. Major new deposits have been found in north-eastern B.C. and are awaiting development.

Most of the coal mines now in production are strip or open-cast operations. The surface overburden must be removed to expose the coal seams beneath, whether through blasting with explosives or by means of giant excavators. Power shovels dig into the coal, which is then trucked to the processing plant.

A few mines are underground, as in the old days. Coal-cutting machines rip into the working face, and the coal reaches the processing plant by conveyor belt. At Sparwood in the Kootenays, the coal in a sloping seam is cut by a jet of water. The method was introduced in the early 1970s, and is said to be more efficient.

Raw coal from both surface and underground workings is screened and washed to reduce its ash content. Then it is dried and stored ready for shipment. Most is exported by way of the Roberts Bank terminal near Vancouver, but there is talk of developing new facilities at Prince Rupert to handle coal deposits found in the north.

The other fossil fuels, oil and natural gas, are found in the north-east of the province. The first commercial discovery of natural gas was made in 1948, close to the Alberta boundary, and of oil in 1952, close to Fort St. John. Today, B.C. produces all of the gas it needs and 25 per cent of its oil.

The oil and gas are transported in separate pipeline systems. The gas is 'scrubbed' (cleaned) at processing plants, and most of it is piped to the lower mainland. Most of the oil goes to Vancouver or across the border into Washington, though some is refined in Prince George and Kamloops.

A winter's view of a surface coal mine in the Eastern Kootenay, at work 24 hours a day to supply metallurgical coal to Japanese markets.

FISHING

Other species help, but the real strengths of B.C.'s fisheries are salmon, herring, and halibut. Salmon alone contribute more than 60 per cent of the value of the catch, and herring provide a further 20 per cent.

The salmon fishery has a long history. Early in the nineteenth century the Hudson's Bay Company exported salted salmon to Europe. The first canning plant, at Annieville on the Fraser river, went into production in 1870. As the industry developed, canning plants appeared in every major inlet along the coast.

Today, processing plants are concentrated in the lower mainland and around Prince Rupert. Three salmon species — sockeyes, pinks, and chums — are used only for canning. Cohos are canned, smoked, frozen, or sold fresh. Chinooks, by far the largest and most impressive species, are sold fresh or frozen.

Most of the salmon are caught as they migrate to their spawning grounds after reaching maturity deep in the ocean. With the United States, Canada imposes a 'surf-line' in coastal waters to limit the operations of net fishermen. Only trollers, small vessels towing six lines of hooks, may catch salmon outside the surf-line.

Each troller is equipped with four long poles to keep its lines separated. The two bow poles trail single lines, and those amidships carry two apiece. When

Pacific Salmon

Canada's five species of Pacific salmon differ in size and habits, but in general their life histories are similar. Sockeyes, pinks, chums, chinooks, and cohos all begin as eggs laid in gravel beds in fall and incubate during the months of winter.

In late winter the eggs hatch as 'alevins,' with huge eyes and an orange yolk sack that provides their food. The alevins grow rapidly, and in May or June emerge from the gravel as free-swimming 'fry.' Still tiny, the fry easily fall prey to larger fish. Pinks and chums that survive swim directly to the sea, but other species remain in the stream or move into a lake for a year.

Sockeyes, chinooks, and cohos migrate to the sea as 'smolts' in their second spring. Sockeyes feed on plankton and crustaceans like pinks and chums, but chinooks and cohos eat smaller fish. Each species gains weight rapidly until it is mature, then begins its long journey to the place where it was spawned.

The fish that reach fresh water stop eating and begin living on stored body fat. Pinks head for spawning grounds only a short distance from the sea, but the largest species must travel up to 1500 km or even farther to reach their birthplace. On the way they must overcome rapids and evade inland

Fisheries conservation officers net salmon in a spawning channel. The salmon will be taken to a hatchery, where their eggs will be fertilized and young fry will be raised under controlled conditions.

fishermen and hungry bears.

On their spawning grounds the fish pair off. By flapping their tails over the bottom, the females dig nests or 'redds,' cavities up to 40 cm deep. They lay eggs in thousands, and the males fertilize them with 'milt.' Then the females cover the eggs by excavating further redds a short distance upstream. Soon after spawning, both sexes die, and their bodies drift in the current.

Fishermen haul in a purse seine bulging with salmon, intercepted within the 'surf-line' imposed by Canada and the United States to conserve salmon stocks.

a fish takes a hook, the pole bends and the fisherman hauls in the line. He aims to catch chinooks and cohos for the fresh market, so he takes care not to damage them.

Trollers take about 25 per cent of all the salmon caught. The remainder are taken by purse seiners and gillnetters. A seiner aims to surround the fish with a net, then purse its bottom and haul the fish to the surface. A gillnetter sets nets to hang in the water and catch fish by the gills.

The salmon fishery occurs in summer. Most of the fishermen also take part in the lucrative herring fisheries of fall and February. Before 1968, herring were fished to make fish meal and oil, but their numbers declined so drastically that the fishery was closed. Since then stocks have recovered, but they are fished for different purposes.

In fall, the herring's oil content is high, and they are netted as food for human consumption. In February they approach the shore to spawn, and are fished for their roe, which is a delicacy in Japan. The carcasses of herring caught in February are processed as fish meal.

Both gillnetters and seiners take part in the herring fishery, and to a lesser extent so do trollers and groundfish trawlers that catch fish in large, bag-like nets hauled behind them. At other times of the year the trawlers pursue sole, cod, and flounder, but most halibut are caught by longliners.

Like gillnetters that suspend their nets from floating buoys, longliners pay out many kilometres of line carrying up to 3000 baited hooks. After some hours the line is hauled in mechanically, and fish are recovered as they come over the side. Then the lines are rebaited and returned to the sea.

Smaller longliners work inshore, but larger vessels often venture far out to sea. Since 1977, Canada's fishing waters have been extended to 200 nautical miles (about 370 km). The increased limit is helping groundfish stocks to recover after years of overfishing by the fleets of other nations.

Gillnetters set a long, weighted net that hangs from buoys and catches fish by the gills.

MANUFACTURING

Forest producers excepted, the great majority of B.C.'s manufacturers are in the lower mainland. They range from tiny one-man concerns serving the local consumer market to large enterprises that export worldwide.

These enterprises produce everything from furniture to fishing tackle, from smoked salmon to sound systems. Some add value to raw materials produced in the province, some must import their raw materials from outside, but together they provide an impressive counterweight to the industrial muscle of Eastern Canada.

Inevitably, the manufacturing sector as a whole is dominated by lumber and newsprint. The two provide half the value of all shipments. Food and beverages are in third place, among them commodities like sugar that are processed locally, though brought in from other countries.

The food and beverages sector is as diverse as the mining industry. There are

A log is mounted on a lathe and rotated against a cutting edge to produce the veneer used to make plywood.

Construction

Shopping centres, power dams, industrial plants, residential units — all are grist to the mill for B.C.'s construction industry. Most developments are in the lower mainland, but there have been ambitious projects all over the province.

The construction industry is more diverse than most, and the companies involved tend to specialize. Some concentrate on housing, some on commercial projects and institutions like hospitals. A third group tackles complex industrial plants like oil refineries. A fourth engineers highways and bridges.

Architects, engineers, and some 15 separate trades are represented in the industry — a measure of its complexity. Most of their time is spent on new construction, but sometimes they bring new life to old — for example, in restoring Vancouver's Gastown and the waterfront area in Victoria.

All over the province, the scenery demands the best that architects and the construction industry can provide. Inevitably there are eyesores, among them some of the pulpmills, but for the most part standards are high. Not the least accomplishment is the Vancouver skyline, usually regarded as one of the world's most beautiful.

The construction industry plays a major role in B.C.'s economy, partly as an employer and partly as a means of generating work for other industries.

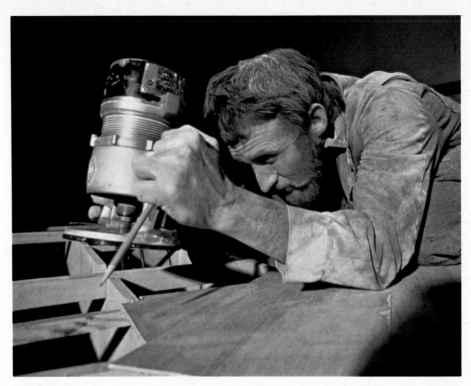

Industries like this furniture factory help to supply B.C.'s consumer market, but many items must be imported from outside the province.

meat packers in Kamloops, dairy producers on Vancouver Island, fish canneries in Prince Rupert. Beer is brewed from Creston hops, and Okanagan grapes are blended to make British Columbian wine.

Food processors cater both to local consumers and to the export market. However, consumer manufacturing as a whole falls far short of meeting the province's needs. Labour costs are high, and it is often cheaper to bring in goods from Eastern Canada, the United States, Europe, or South-East Asia than to make them locally.

An example is the clothing industry. Manufacturers tend to leave the mass-market to imports, and instead concentrate on high-price, high-quality garments that local consumers will appreciate. Vancouverites in particular have a high sense of fashion, and the local industry can meet their needs.

The same is true of furniture and recreational products. Local goods must be supplemented by those brought in from outside. With electrical and electronic items, however, the province can hold its own. Communications equipment, control systems, and other high-technology products are sold to many countries.

In the electronics field, technological excellence is what matters. The same is true of industrial equipment. Local manufacturers cater to food processors and the mining industry, but the province's specialty is sawmill machinery. Barkers, trimmers, edgers, and many other devices are exported in large quantities.

Also encouraged by the resource industries, several manufacturers produce heavy-duty trucks and other vehicles for use off the highways. Another style of transportation is represented at two shipyards, one in North Vancouver and one in Esquimalt on Vancouver Island, and in boatyards that build tugs, barges, and fishing vessels.

The shipyards and equipment man-

ufacturers use substantial quantities of steel, and so does the construction industry. As yet the province has no real steel industry beyond a rolling mill, though there has been talk of developing one. During most of the 1970s world steel prices were so depressed that there was no need.

Chemical industries, however, are

another story. A number of small-scale fertilizer and explosives plants are already in production, and petrochemicals are a possibility. Once Alberta's primary petrochemicals producers are in their stride, B.C. will be able to develop 'downstream' plants producing plastics and other commodities for the local market and the world.

Industries employing high technology have proved profitable in B.C. This is a company making complex diving equipment for undersea exploration.

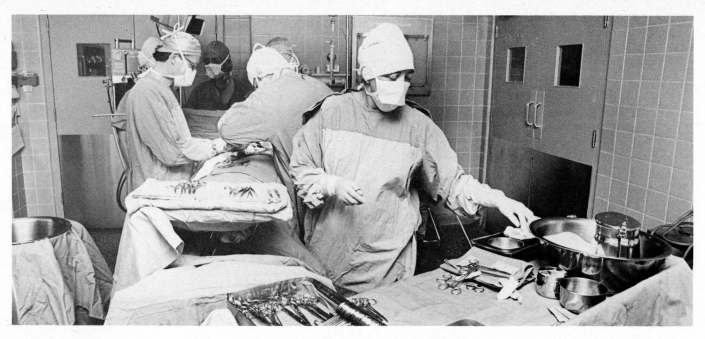

LABOUR RELATIONS

More than anywhere else in Canada, people in British Columbia like to take sides. It seems to be part of the provincial character that issues are seen in black and white, and everyone makes it their business to express an opinion.

Often the opinion is deliberately exaggerated and emotions run wild. Neither side to a dispute is prepared to back down, and the result is a stalemate. Many good ideas have to be dropped because of the weight of feeling against them, though to be fair, many bad ideas are defeated too.

Confrontation is traditional in provincial politics, the arts, and many other fields. Above all it is traditional in labour relations. More than half of the workforce is organized in trade unions, a far higher proportion than in Canada as a whole. Even more remarkable, the employers are organized too.

Labour relations have been a problem in British Columbia since the early days. The province attracted independent spirits who valued their rights and were prepared to fight for them. Even before 1900, hardrock miners and others were forming unions to fight for job security, better wages, and industrial safety.

Strikes became part of British Columbia's way of life and have remained so. Often they were ended only through the intervention of the courts. Labour relations steadily worsened, and the province gained the reputation of being one of the most strike-ridden areas of North America.

Labour troubles figured large in the defeat of W. A. C. Bennett's Social Crediters in 1972, and their replacement by the New Democrats led by David Barrett. The NDP immediately ordered an inquiry into labour matters, and in 1973 introduced a comprehensive labour code.

The code was to be implemented by a labour relations board (LRB), distinct

Under British Columbia's labour laws, public servants providing essential services in hospitals have only limited rights to strike. Similar provisions cover the police and firefighters.

Labour demonstrations and strike pickets have been a familiar sight in B.C. Here, representatives of a seamen's union protest the absence of a Canadian merchant marine.

Strikes and Lockouts

B.C.'s labour code enshrines two basic freedoms. One is the employees' right to withhold their labour as a means of bargaining, providing they give due warning. The other is the employers' right to lock them out.

Neither side may take action while bound by a collective agreement, but otherwise there are few restrictions. Once out, the employees will probably picket the employers' premises to publicize their grievances. Besides, the picket line will discourage other workers from supporting the employers or from taking the employees' jobs.

Picket lines are a familiar sight in British Columbia, in spite of the Labour Relations Board. Only when discussions have broken down will one or other side resort to the LRB for help. Even then the strike or lockout will continue until the dispute is resolved.

There is a notable exception to the right to strike. The provincial cabinet can impose a 90-day suspension period on strike action involving essential services like the police, hospitals, and firefighters. Alternatively, the LRB can sanction a rotating strike that leaves an adequate number of key personnel on duty.

Newspaper typesetters locked out by their employers picket their offices in Vancouver. A picket line advertises the protesters' complaints and discourages other workers from supporting the employers.

from the courts and independent of the government. The board was to act as referee in disputes between employers and employees, a disinterested third party that sought solutions acceptable to both sides.

Before, many disputes had gone to the courts, which could only decide what was legal and what was not. Unions had tended to distrust the courts, for decisions nearly always went against them. The LRB was designed to be flexible — expected to go all out for industrial peace almost regardless of the letter of the law.

The idea of the board was greeted enthusiastically by the employers and by the public at large, but ironically the unions were not impressed and marched on the legislature in protest. Several years passed before the board gained general acceptance, but in 1977 fewer workdays were lost through disputes than in any year since 1965.

The LRB consists of a chairman and six vice-chairmen (half of them lawyers) who work full-time, and about 18 part-time 'wingers' who assist them in deciding disputes. Usually wingers are invited to serve on the board because of their special knowledge of labour or of management.

Much of the LRB's work is completed before any hearings are necessary. Formal applications can be dealt with by its clerical staff, and minor disputes are often settled by LRB officers who act as go-betweens. More serious disputes come before an LRB panel for a decision.

A panel can consist of a single vice-chairman, or of enough people to ensure that it is neutral — typically, a vice-chairman and two wingers reflecting the opposing interests. The panel's decision is binding but may be appealed, in which case it is heard by an entirely fresh panel.

In extreme cases, the board can go as far as disciplining one of the parties and awarding damages for injury. As a last resort, it can refer its decisions to the courts for judicial confirmation. Some decisions have been controversial, but both employers and employees have accepted them, and most of the old-style confrontation is being avoided.

Mica dam, one of three built in accordance with the Columbia river treaty signed by Canada and the United States. Mica is the only one of the three used to generate electricity.

A provincial utility, B.C. Hydro generates most of B.C.'s electrical power, but several large industries, like smelters and refineries, draw their supplies from private sources.

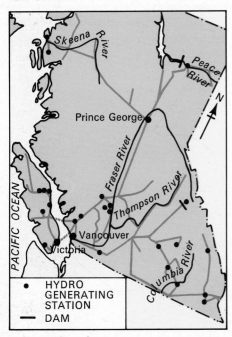

HYDRO GENERATING STATION
DAM

ENERGY

Most of B.C.'s crude oil is imported from Alberta, but it supplies its other energy needs from within the province. Electricity and natural gas carry much of the load, coal reserves are immense, and forest producers rely on waste wood known as 'hog fuel.'

A small proportion of the electricity is produced by thermal generating stations, but more than 90 per cent comes from water power. There have been hydroelectric generating stations in the lower mainland since early in the century, but the most powerful are in the north and to the east.

Until the late 1960s, the largest hydroelectric operation in the province was the Kemano plant near Kitimat, producing power for the aluminum smelter. Four hydro stations on the Kootenay river were linked with the smelter at Trail. All these facilities remain independent of B.C. Hydro, the provincial utility.

Before B.C. Hydro was formed, electricity was supplied by a number of small utilities active in particular regions. All but one have been absorbed by B.C.

Hydro, which has also developed major plants of its own. Most of its generating stations are in two areas, the Columbia river system in the east and the Peace river district in the north.

The Columbia flows from Canada into the United States, and in the past caused major floods in Washington and Oregon. As a result, in 1964 Canada and the United States signed the Columbia River Treaty, under which Canada undertook to construct three major dams to regulate the river's flow.

B.C. Hydro undertook to build the three dams. At one site, Mica, the utility has developed one of the world's largest underground powerhouses. Huge turbines have been installed, rotated by water falling down steep penstocks. The turbines spin at high speed and turn shafts connected to powerful generators.

With the Mica dam controlling the river's flow, it was feasible to build a second large powerhouse near Revelstoke, 93 km downstream. At the same time, B.C. Hydro built new installations on the Kootenay and Pend d'Oreille rivers, both tributaries of the Columbia.

To harness the Peace, B.C. Hydro

Additional generators are installed in the huge underground powerhouse attached to Mica dam on the Columbia river.

built the W.A.C. Bennett dam, which was completed in 1967. The dam created the Williston reservoir, the largest lake in the province and the source of power for another huge underground powerhouse. A second powerhouse is being built a few kilometres downstream.

There are several other river sites with major potential, but they will probably not be developed. In some cases dams would interfere with salmon spawning runs, in others they would be uneconomic. B.C. Hydro has been looking at alternative sources of energy, notably coal.

Even conservative estimates suggest that B.C. has enough coal to provide power for centuries to come. Already some thermal coal is being mined for export, but B.C. Hydro is planning to build generating stations beside the deposits. One especially favourable site is Hat Creek near Lillooet, and a second is the East Kootenays.

Another promising idea is the use of geothermal power — steam or hot water trapped far beneath the earth's surface. The steam can be tapped to spin turbines, just as in a conventional thermal generating plant. Several possible sites have been identified, but as yet it is not economic to develop them.

All the existing generating stations are linked to B.C. Hydro's power grid, which reaches most communities. Some outlying regions and several of the islands are served by diesel generators, but 70 per cent of Vancouver Island's power is transmitted from the mainland by undersea cable.

As yet little electricity has been sold to the United States, apart from power generated south of the border but belonging to B.C. in terms of the Columbia River Treaty. If new sales of electricity can be arranged, it will be worthwhile to develop the coal-fuelled stations proposed for Hat Creek and elsewhere.

Besides electricity, B.C. Hydro distributes most of the natural gas con-

sumed in the province. Local oil meets only 25 per cent of requirements, so the remainder must be brought in from Alberta. These conventional forms of energy are supplemented by hog fuel, burned by forest producers to power and heat their plants.

Energy specialists calculate that hog fuel produces more than 10 per cent of all the energy consumed in British Columbia. That compares with about 20 per cent produced by natural gas, 18 per cent by electricity, 50 per cent by oil, and only 1 per cent by coal.

The generating station at the Kootenay canal, midway between Nelson and Castlegar.

TRANSPORTATION

In its day, the Cariboo Road built by military engineers during the 1860s was the wonder of British Columbia. It stretched nearly 650 km from Yale to the Cariboo goldfields and was constructed so solidly that parts of the original road are still in use today.

During the goldrush, traffic on the Cariboo Road was heavy. At Yale, supplies were loaded on mule trains of from 16 to 48 animals. Progress was slow, and it took at least 18 days to reach the diggings. A round trip took more than a month, and most packers could make only three trips a year.

Wheeled traffic used the road to carry passengers, but it was to remain the only highway into the interior until the 1920s. There were local roads in the lower mainland and on Vancouver Island, but long-distance transport needs were met by the railroads. By 1915, three major systems were in operation.

One of these systems was the CPR, entering B.C. by way of the Kicking Horse pass and reaching the sea at Vancouver. Both the Canadian Northern and Grand Trunk Pacific lines entered the province through the Yellowhead pass. The Canadian Northern was routed to Vancouver, but the GTP went to Prince Rupert.

The GTP lost money from the start, and passed into the hands of the Dominion government. The Canadian Northern did better, but in 1923, it, too, was absorbed by a federal Crown corporation, Canadian National Railways. The CPR survived and has prospered with the times.

Today, both CN and CP Rail rely heavily on super-long trains that carry freight in bulk. Such trains may extend more than two kilometres and are pulled by up to 13 locomotives. The commodities moved include coal, grain, potash, ore concentrates, forest products, automobiles, containers, and liquid petroleum.

Besides the two major systems, there are several lesser railroads in the province. British Columbia Railway extends

Lions Gate suspension bridge spans Burrard Inlet in Vancouver and is one of the world's most spectacular.

The Alaska Highway starts at Dawson Creek and traverses forests and mountains on its way to the north.

The Alaska Highway starts at Dawson Creek and traverses forests and mountains on its way to the north.

from North Vancouver to Fort Nelson by way of Prince George, interlocking with CN's line to Prince Rupert and with Northern Alberta Railways. Ultimately the BCR will be extended into the north-west.

Most of the province's rail routes follow well-defined transport corridors through the mountains, many of them river valleys. From the early days settlements developed along the tracks, but there was little effort to open up the hinterland as happened on the prairies.

As a result, large areas of B.C. are virtually inaccessible except by air. Most of the highways use the same corridors as the railroads, and that is also true of sub-surface pipelines and overhead powerlines. Even then, mountains, gorges, and rivers have posed enormous problems of engineering.

In many places construction crews have had to blast tunnels — among them, seven on the Fraser canyon section of Highway 1, which follows the route of the Cariboo Road. Elsewhere they have built bridges, and the province now possesses several of the most spectacular and elegant in North America.

Some of the bridges are suspended — for instance, the Peace river bridge near Hudson's Hope and the famous Lions Gate in Vancouver. Some are single arches (for instance, Alexandria bridge over the Fraser), some continuous-span (Columbia river bridge at Kinnaird), some cantilevered (Agassiz-Rosedale over the Fraser).

Channeled through the transport corridors, some highways take motorists far out of their way. British Columbians have long since learned the value of air transportation, whether by scheduled services or by smaller aircraft that can land wherever there is a runway or a stretch of clear water.

General aviation is unusually well developed in B.C., not least to serve Vancouver Island and the Queen Char-

lottes. So is the operation of large commercial carriers like Air Canada and CP Air, which has its headquarters in Vancouver, and the regional carrier Pacific Western Airlines.

CP Air's services are local, national, and international. Among its destina-

tions are Australia, the Far East, and South America. Air Canada concentrates on transcontinental services and flights to Europe, the Middle East, and the Caribbean. Pacific Western links communities in British Columbia, Alberta, and the Northwest Territories.

British Columbia Railway runs from North Vancouver to Fort Nelson in northern B.C. by way of Prince George. There are plans to extend the railroad to Alaska.

The *Queen of Prince Rupert*, **flagship of the B.C. ferry fleet, cruises the Inside Passage on its way to Prince Rupert.**

Horseshoe Pier, a busy ferry terminal near Vancouver that serves Vancouver Island and smaller islands lying offshore.

Ferry Services

Nearly one in six British Columbians live on Vancouver Island, the Queen Charlottes, and smaller islands in Georgia Strait. The islanders have ready access to and from the mainland by way of a remarkable fleet of ferries that operate all through the year.

Before 1960, Vancouver Island and Vancouver were linked by two private shipping companies. In 1958 the seamen of one of these companies went on strike, and only last-minute intervention by the provincial government kept the other one in service. Plainly the existing services were extremely vulnerable, and something had to be done.

As a result, the B.C. government entered the ferry business. In 1960 two vessels were constructed to sail between Victoria and the lower mainland. Soon more vessels were acquired to serve smaller islands. The new fleet carried its one-millionth passenger in June 1962, and its one-millionth vehicle in April 1963.

Since then, the fleet has expanded to more than 20 vessels, nearly all of them crowned 'queens' of the destinations they serve. Between them they travel over a dozen routes, the busiest of them being Vancouver-Victoria and Vancouver-Nanaimo, and the longest being the winter journey from Vancouver to Prince Rupert — 483 nautical miles.

Many of the ferries were built in B.C. Besides, as demand has increased, several of them have been modified. Some now have a suspended 'platform' deck to hold more vehicles, and some have been 'stretched' — cut in half and lengthened by the addition of a new midsection that adds nearly 30 m to the original.

The flagship of the fleet is the *Queen of Prince Rupert*, especially designed to travel B.C.'s famous inside passage and launched in 1965. In summer the ship sails from the north end of Vancouver Island, in winter from Vancouver. Like its sisters it carries passengers and vehicles and is much in demand with tourists.

Besides the government ferries, private companies link Nanaimo with Vancouver and Victoria with Seattle, Washington. Freight is shipped to Victoria and Nanaimo aboard self propelled rail barges, and more barges operate between Prince Rupert and the Queen Charlottes. Small coastal freighters link ports from Victoria to Prince Rupert.

THE PORTS

A century ago, British Columbia's leading ports were Victoria and New Westminster. Vancouver's Burrard Inlet was still a forested backwater, ignored except by occasional sailing ships calling to load lumber from its two sawmills.

Then came news that the Canadian Pacific Railway had selected Burrard Inlet as its western terminus. A town developed, and the railroad built wharves to serve ships sailing to and from the Far East. From 1887, there were regular sailings between Vancouver and Japan.

Vancouver steadily gained in status as part of a transport system that spanned the world. Passengers from the Far East landed in Vancouver, crossed Canada by train, then sailed the Atlantic to reach Europe. Meanwhile, other companies introduced mail and passenger services between Vancouver and Australia.

In 1914 the Panama Canal was opened, and B.C. had an easy sea route to Europe. In 1915 a second transcontinental railroad reached Vancouver and the CPR had competition. In 1923 an American steamer carried the first bulk shipment of prairie grain from Vancouver to Britain, and a huge new market proved feasible.

Vancouver has grown with B.C., and today its port is the busiest in Canada and one of the most significant in North America. New Westminster and Victoria are in its shadow, and so are its old rivals San Francisco and Seattle. Each year the port expands, developing new facilities to meet the demands of trade.

Until the early 1960s, most of the freight passing through Vancouver was general cargo moved by all-purpose ships. Grain was the only bulk commodity. Today, most cargo is handled in bulk — coal, grain, potash, sulphur, phosphate rock — or stuffed into containers that need not be 'destuffed' on the way to their destination.

Burrard Inlet is now ringed by special loading berths designed for these commodities. Large terminal elevators spout grain into ships' holds. Potash and ore concentrate are piled high until required. Containers are stacked at the Vanterm yard on the inlet's south shore, until huge carriers load them on to specially designed ships.

Lynnterm is a new general cargo terminal on the inlet's north shore. It specializes in forest products and steel, but is also equipped to handle containers. Coal, however, is railed to Roberts Bank, an artificial island 35 km south of Vancouver that can be enlarged as required.

B.C.'s other ports see only a fraction of the cargo that passes through the province. Victoria, Nanaimo, and New Westminster all have deep-sea berths, but deal only with general commodities, particularly forest products. Vancouver's only potential rival is Prince Rupert far to the north.

From its foundation, Prince Rupert was meant to become a major port. Its harbour is as spacious and sheltered as Burrard Inlet, and its special advantage is that it lies even closer to the Far East. However, for most of its existence it has served only as a relief port, storing grain for which Vancouver has no room.

Now that is changing. For some time the government of Alberta has wanted Prince Rupert developed as a natural outlet for the prairies. Albertan funds have made it possible to build a new grain terminal at the northern port, and also facilities for handling coal and forest products. It may be that Prince Rupert's hour has come.

The Port of Vancouver's Vanterm serves container traffic, loading and unloading specialized vessels and storing the containers until required for onward shipping.

TRADE AND COMMERCE

Roughly half of what British Columbia produces is consumed locally. About 42 per cent is exported, chiefly to the United States and Europe, and the remainder goes to other parts of Canada.

That pattern suggests the south and east, yet British Columbians have always looked first to the west. Both Vancouver and Prince Rupert were founded as 'gateways to the Orient,' catering to trade relations first established after Captain Cook discovered the Nootka sea otters.

Of course, most of British Columbia's trade with the Far East involves other provinces. Albertan coal, Saskatchewan potash, Manitoban wheat destined for Japan or China must be routed through B.C. ports, and so must Japanese automobiles, Korean textiles, and Hong Kong radios intended for the whole of Canada.

B.C.'s exports to Japan include metallurgical coal, copper ore, lumber, herring roe, pulp, and aluminum ingots from Kitimat. Besides automobiles and other consumer goods, the province imports quantities of iron and steel — supplied more cheaply than from Eastern Canada or the United States.

From Australia and New Zealand, B.C. imports meat, canned and dried fruit, alumina for smelting, and raw sugar. In return the province exports canned salmon, forest products, refined aluminum, and sulphur. Other markets across the Pacific include Taiwan, Singapore, Thailand, Malaysia, and Indonesia.

To the United States, B.C. exports not only by sea, but also by road, rail, pipeline, and even air freight. Lumber, pulp, newsprint, and plywood are the most valuable exports, and besides them crude petroleum, natural gas, ore concentrates, refined non-ferrous metals, fish products, cattle, fruit, and manufactured goods.

Most imports from the United States are manufactured, but they range from seasonal vegetables and citrus fruits to advanced technical products like computers and aircraft. A similar variety of goods is brought in from the rest of Canada, and B.C. reciprocates with lumber, fruit, fish products, and manufactured goods.

To Europe go asbestos from Cassiar, lumber and newsprint, fish and fruit, copper concentrate, and coal. In the past, most of these goods went to Britain, but that country's share has declined, while the rest of the European Economic Community takes more. Besides, Warsaw Pact nations like Rumania have become customers too.

Most of these products are routed

Saskatchewan Wheat Pool's terminal grain elevator in the Port of Vancouver. Most of the grain shipped from Vancouver is bound for the Far East, particularly China.

The Lynnterm general cargo terminal in the Port of Vancouver, one of North America's busiest. In the distance are the highrise towers of Vancouver's downtown core.

through Vancouver, and that is where nearly all of B.C.'s resource producers have their head offices. Mining companies, pulp and paper producers, fish processors, and transportation agents are located within a stone's throw of each other in the central business district.

With few exceptions these companies are listed on the Vancouver Stock Exchange, the busiest in Western Canada. There, daily trading in the shares of local companies reflects the vagaries of international markets. Sophisticated telecommunications keep Vancouver in touch with the rest of North America and the world outside.

Vancouver's business community is firmly in control of developments in the south of the province, but in the north the picture is less clear. Prince George is the chief distribution centre for the north, but north-eastern communities receive a high proportion of their goods and services from Edmonton in Alberta.

Of course, the Peace river country has close geographic and cultural ties with Albertan communities across the boundary, and the petroleum industry of the north-east is an extension of Alberta's. Even so, some British Columbians accuse the Albertans of empire-building, particularly now that they are helping to develop Prince Rupert as their special outlet to the sea.

The Travellers

Tourism is B.C.'s third largest industry after forestry and mining. Trail riders, motorists, fishermen, conventioneers, couples on honeymoon — the travellers fall into many categories, but all have time to spare and money to spend.

The province has attracted visitors since the building of the CPR, but only since the 1950s have they been arriving in large numbers. Some seek wilderness, some want popular resorts and organized activity, but the revenue they bring makes it worthwhile to develop new facilities that in turn increase the tourist traffic.

Barkerville, the gold rush town of the Cariboo, was reconstructed expressly for the industry. So was Fort Steele near Cranbrook, a former Mountie post in the Kootenays. Scenic routes like the highway through Rogers Pass have no other economic justification, and the same goes for many of the provincial parks.

The travellers who benefit most from the facilities are the British Columbians themselves. They and other Canadians account for two-thirds of all travel in the province. Americans have discovered B.C. too, and the 'offshore' visitors are mostly from Japan, Britain, France, and West Germany.

Individual cases vary greatly, but it is fair to take motorists as typical visitors. The industry calculates that they spend up to 30 per cent of their total outlay on food, about 25 per cent

on travel, 20 per cent on lodging, perhaps 15 per cent on shopping, six per cent on entertainment, and four per cent on personal services.

The lower mainland receives the lion's share of the tourism dollars, with Victoria and the Okanagan close behind. Increasingly, the industry's benefits are being spread to other regions, too — from dude ranches in the Kootenays to fishing camps in Atlin, far away in B.C.'s north-west corner.

B.C. tourism authorities divide the province into seven regions as follows: 1. Vancouver Island; 2. South-western B.C.; 3. Okanagan; 4. Kootenays; 5. Thompson–Shuswap; 6. Cariboo–Chilcotin; 7. Yellowhead-Highway 16; 8. Peace River–Liard.

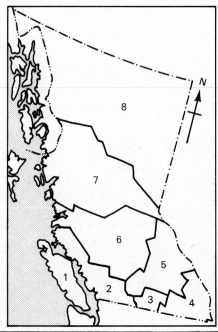

VANCOUVER

Some travellers approach Vancouver by land and some by air, but the luckiest enter in from the sea. For them, the Lions Gate suspension bridge is an arch of welcome, and the narrows of Burrard Inlet open into one of the world's most enchanting harbours.

Each summer Vancouver sees a procession of luxury cruise ships, some based in the port and some calling there on the way between San Francisco and Alaska. Thousands of passengers disembark at the terminal near the foot of Granville Street, the busy thoroughfare that divides the city into east and west.

As soon as they step ashore, the cruise passengers are surrounded by the highrise towers of Vancouver's business district — hotels, offices, stores, and apartment blocks. Many of the highrises offer exceptional views of the inlet and the mountains that overlook it, and of North Vancouver on the opposite shore.

Often ships give their passengers only a day to see the city. Some will cross to North Vancouver on a sea-bus, a neat catamaran ferry that makes the trip in seven minutes. Those wanting a more extensive look at the port will board the *Beaver*, a reconstruction of a famous paddle-steamer that served the Hudson's Bay Company for nearly 40 years.

Some passengers will hire a car. Grouse Mountain and its cableways are only 20 minutes from the city centre, and the summit provides a breathtaking view of all Vancouver. Much closer is Stanley Park, a spacious peninsula set aside as a military reserve during the 1860s and later turned into a place of recreation.

Stanley Park is Vancouver's playground. Surrounded by an 11 km sea wall, it holds a zoo, sporting facilities, and 500 ha of natural woodlands. Besides, it is the home of Canada's premier aquarium, an entertainment centre and research laboratory all in one which holds nearly 9000 specimens of sea life

Granville Street cuts downtown Vancouver in half, and offers a glimpse of the mountains across Burrard Inlet. The street is closed to all traffic except buses.

Chinatown

There are Chinese Canadians all over Vancouver, but 80 000 of them live in the city's Chinatown, the second largest in North America after San

Vancouver's Chinatown is the second largest in North America, and its restaurants and stores are a major draw for Vancouverites and visitors alike.

Francisco's. Chinatown has existed since the 1880s, when anti-oriental feeling among whites compelled the Chinese to live together for their own protection.

Most of the Chinese had been brought to British Columbia to work on railroad construction. When the CPR was completed, many decided not to return home. They and their descendants were resented and often harassed by whites until World War II, when suddenly public opinion changed and China was recognized as 'a brave Asian ally.'

Today, Chinatown is one of Vancouver's great assets. Its stores carry imported camphorwood, jade, ivory, and silk, not to mention bamboo. Its restaurants, popular with both Vancouverites and visitors, represent every major Chinese cuisine except Fukian — Szechuian, Peking or Mandarin, Cantonese, Hunan, and Shanghai.

Some stores stock traditional Chinese medicines, and there are practising acupuncturists, but many younger Chinese have little interest in them. The same is true of the Chinese language, for most now speak English. Even so, games of mahjong remain the favourite leisure pastime, particularly as the whole family can join in.

Many of Chinatown's residents are third or fourth generation Canadians and proud of it, but most retain links with relatives in the old country, even if they have never met them. On their behalf, Chinatown banks dispatch large sums of money to less fortunate cousins across the Pacific.

A commuter sea-bus links downtown Vancouver with the north shore across Burrard Inlet.

from the Pacific and elsewhere.

There are many more places to be seen — the campuses of the University of British Columbia and of Simon Fraser University in Burnaby; the H. R. Mac-Millan planetarium; the Bloedel conservatory, which simulates three different climatic zones — desert, rain forest, and tropical forest; and the world's longest foot suspension bridge, spanning the gorge of the Capilano river in North Vancouver.

For many visitors, Vancouver's brightest attraction is Gastown, a daring exercise in urban renewal that has rescued many of the city's old buildings from oblivion. Gastown is where Vancouver began, and was named after 'Gassy Jack' Deighton, who landed there in the 1860s and set up a tent tavern to sell whisky to visiting sailors.

'Gassy Jack' — the name reflected his taste for conversation — died in 1875, by which time Gastown was officially known as Granville, after a British colonial secretary. Even so, the old name stuck, and was still in use in 1886 when the CPR arrived and the settlement was incorporated under the new name of Vancouver.

Today, much of Gastown is a pedestrian precinct that blends ancient with modern. Neat brick walkways are lined by aged warehouses and office blocks that have had a facelift. Now they hold restaurants, discos, specialty stores, and art galleries, and Gastown is lively at all hours of the day and much of the night, too.

The cruise ship passenger cannot hope to sample in a single day all that Vancouver has to offer. Theatre, symphony, the Pacific National Exhibition, sailing, water-skiing, snow-skiing — the

list goes on and on. Even Vancouverites have to be selective, but most of them manage to make the most of a lifestyle that is the envy of the rest of Canada.

This statue of 'Gassy Jack,' often thought of as Vancouver's founder, stands in the heart of Gastown, which grew around his saloon.

THE REGIONS

Geographic features are so prominent in British Columbia that the various regions are more clearly defined than anywhere else in Canada. So are the communities that they contain, for each has a personality of its own.

Take the East and West Kootenay, in the south-east. Together, the mountainous Kootenays are twice the size of Switzerland and contain even more natural divisions. Communities like Fernie, Invermere, Kimberley, and Revelstoke were founded for quite different reasons and have grown up in isolation.

Fernie, named after a former gold commissioner, was for a long time the region's chief coal-mining centre. In 1908 it was devastated by a forest fire, but it soon recovered. Invermere, close to the site of a fur-trading post founded by David Thompson, thrives as a resort community close to the famous Radium

hot springs.

Kimberley, Canada's highest town, owes its origins to the Sullivan base metals mine. In 1972 its residents added false fronts to many of its buildings and transformed it into a Bavarian village. Revelstoke, once a CPR construction camp, is now a flourishing resort community serving two nearby national parks.

The Kootenays are high, rarified, and exposed. The Okanagan region to the west is sheltered, calm, and fertile. Water from its rivers and lakes is used to irrigate lush orchards rising on the hills, and small towns have expanded rapidly as Canadians from other provinces flood in to share the special lifestyle.

Penticton in the heart of the Okanagan was a ranch in the 1860s, and was laid out as a townsite in 1892. To the north is Peachland, where the Okanagan's peach industry had its start in 1897. Kelowna, now surrounded by orchards and vineyards, grew up around

Prince Rupert was founded as the terminus of a transcontinental railroad. Today it prospers on the strength of its forest industries and its fishing fleet.

an Oblate mission station founded in the 1850s.

Salmon Arm at the head of the Okanagan valley is the gateway to cattle country. Kamloops, capital of the southern interior, was a fur-trading post established in 1812. Now it is best known as a railroad centre and for its meat-packing industry. Merritt to the west balances lumber and livestock with molybdenum from a nearby mine.

Lillooet in the Cariboo, set in scenery that is remarkable even for B.C., was 'mile zero' on the old Cariboo trail. Posting-houses on the trail were labelled according to their distance from Lillooet, and names like 70 Mile House and 100 Mile House have survived B.C.'s switch to kilometres.

Today, the Cariboo is ranching

Grain elevators, some owned by the Alberta Wheat Pool, dominate Dawson Creek in the Peace river country.

country, but Williams Lake, Quesnel, Wells, and a host of ghost towns hold memories of the gold rush years. To the west is the Chilcotin, and a lonely, unpaved highway leads from Williams Lake to Bella Coola on the coast. Bella Coola is famous for the help its inhabitants gave to Alexander Mackenzie in 1793.

The highway north of Williams Lake leads to Prince George, close to B.C.'s geographic centre. Prince George is at the junction of the Nechako and Fraser rivers, and in 1807 Simon Fraser selected the site for a fur-trading post. Now it is the chief distribution centre for most of the north.

There are three pulpmills and several sawmills in Prince George, and forest industries are important all along the highway to Prince Rupert. Vanderhoof, Burns Lake, Smithers, and Terrace are all logging towns, and so is Prince Rupert itself. Besides, Prince Rupert has several fish processing plants.

Prince Rupert received its name on the strength of a national competition held in 1910, organized by the Grand Trunk Pacific railway. Kitimat, accessible from Terrace, was built in the early 1950s to smelt alumina. Southward down the coast is Ocean Falls, a small mill town accessible only by sea or from the air.

North-eastern British Columbia has more in common with the prairies than with the rest of the province. The Peace river country was opened up by settlers at the turn of the century and has prospered through agriculture and the petroleum industry. The Alaska highway begins at Dawson Creek and connects it with Fort St. John and Fort Nelson.

Then there are the islands. The Queen Charlottes alone hold more than 150 of them, though the two largest cover nearly the whole area. The shortest distance between the Queen Charlottes and Prince Rupert is 80 km, and the islands are linked with the mainland by air services and by car ferry.

Prince George in the northern interior, a transportation crossroads and the chief distribution centre for northern B.C.

Vancouver Island is the largest on the west coast of the Americas, just over 450 km long and with a total area of 32 137 km². Its settlements include Nanaimo and Campbell River on the east coast and Port Alberni in the interior. Most of them rely on forest industries, and there is a copper mine near Port Hardy.

These regions contain many scores of communities, but even their combined populations do not come close to balancing the population of the lower mainland. Vancouver, Burnaby, Richmond, New Westminster, and their satellites contain more than half of the province's total, and many more live up the Fraser valley in Matsqui, Chilliwack, and Hope.

Cities and Towns

Statistics Canada conducts a census or mini-census once in five years. In 1976, metropolitan Vancouver (including Burnaby, Richmond, Surrey, and other communities) had a population of 1 166 346, while Greater Victoria held 218 250. Other populations included the following:

Prince George	59 929
Kamloops	58 311
Kelowna	51 955
Nanaimo	40 336
Chilliwack	28 421
Penticton	21 344
Prince Rupert	14 754

VICTORIA

People used to say that Victoria was for the newly wed and the nearly dead. The city was beautiful but sleepy, an enormous garden beside the sea, where time stood still and nothing happened to disturb the tranquillity.

That is no longer true. Victoria is as beautiful as ever, but it has come to life. Young Canadians from the mainland have made homes there, and the city's artistic and social life is flourishing. True, one-quarter of the population are senior citizens, but they, too, make their contributions.

Victoria's experience is not parallelled in Canada — a city that went to sleep for 50 years. In the nineteenth century it had a varied and prosperous career, first in the fur trade, then as a staging post during the years of the Cariboo gold rush, and ultimately as the seat of the provincial government.

The best years of all came in the period of the Klondike and Alaska gold rushes, between 1898 and 1910. Ships called at Victoria to load Nanaimo coal and take on fresh supplies for the goldfields, and local businessmen used their profits to build large mansions that survive as their memorials.

Then the boom ended, and Victoria slipped into limbo. There was no need to build new premises, for those erected before 1910 fulfilled all needs. That was the position until the mid-1960s, when B.C.'s economic boom dragged the capital into the twentieth century.

Understandably, the city fathers were in no way tempted to erase Old Victoria and start again. Several eyesores on the waterfront have been removed, but most of the central zone has been preserved intact. Scores of the original buildings have been restored, and sidewalks have been widened for the greater safety of pedestrians.

Tourism is Victoria's most valuable industry, so there has been a drive to revitalize the downtown business area. Sturdy government offices now rub

Each year two-person crews race inflated inner tubes through the gorge that provides one of Victoria's most beautiful parks.

Victoria's old town has been restored and revitalized for the benefit of the tourist trade, the city's leading industry.

shoulders with attractive restaurants and intriguing boutiques, and often the streets are thronged for 16 hours of the day.

For visitors, many of Victoria's attractions are within a stone's throw of the inner harbour. The ivy-grown façade of the Empress Hotel, built in 1908, is one of the most photographed in Canada and neatly complements the legislative building near by. The two were the work of the same architect, Francis Rattenbury.

Between them is B.C.'s provincial museum, one of the most progressive in North America. History is brought to life in displays that feature realistic sounds and smells as well as sights, and a special gallery contains the provincial collection of west coast Indian art and artifacts.

Beacon Hill Park, also close to the inner harbour, offers a taste of Vancouver Island's flora and fauna and magnificent views of the sea. For many visitors, Victoria's outstanding attraction is Butchart Gardens in Saanich, really four gardens in one and created from worked-out gravel pits. They have been open to the public since 1904.

There are many other attractions for visitors, but Victorians have a favourite of their own — the gorge, a tidal inlet that bisects the city and has been developed as a park. Each year, Victorians congregate there for the city's strangest race — two-person crews paddling giant inner tubes as if they were canoes.

The English Connection

For much of the year, downtown Victoria is inundated by cheerful Americans who have crossed from Washington in search of Old England. They tour the city in double-decker buses, search stores for English china and woollens, and take tea at the Empress Hotel.

Victorians are philosophic about the invasion because it helps their tourist industry, but most agree that it is a charade. The city's 'Englishness' came from the British Empire, not Britain itself. Victoria's exceptional climate and surroundings proved irresistible to retired colonial administrators from India and the Far East.

In Victoria, the old colonials could afford to live far more lavishly than in Britain. Besides, Vancouver Island was itself a former colony, and had an atmosphere that the China hands could relate to. It was they who set the tone of elegant gentility that survives to the present.

Of course, the British Empire has dissolved, and with it the colonial administration. People still retire to Victoria, but they are more likely to come from Saskatchewan than from the Punjab. The English connection is a memory kept alive for visitors, for Victoria is as Canadian as any city in the country.

The Empress Hotel is still Victoria's best-known landmark, and each afternoon visitors flock to take tea in its spacious lobby.

GOVERNMENT

On a national level, British Columbians elect 28 members of parliament to the House of Commons in Ottawa. They are also represented by six senators, and normally at least one British Columbian serves in the federal cabinet, while another is a judge of the Supreme Court of Canada.

Even so, Ottawa is a long way from Vancouver and Victoria, and British Columbians tend to be cynical about what happens there. Many feel that the federal government both misunderstands and mistreats them and tend to view Ottawa as an agency of Ontario and Quebec, rather than as the servant of Canada as a whole.

To them, government is Victoria, a

The picturesque facade of Victoria's city hall hides a modern annex that has been built on behind it.

The Courts

Victorians would deny it vigorously, but unofficially B.C. has two capitals. The provincial legislature and the executive-cum-administration are in Victoria, but the judiciary has its headquarters in Vancouver.

The mainland has been the focus of judicial activity since the time of the Cariboo gold rush. To the consternation of American miners used to the rule of the gun, the British sent a judge to keep the peace. The judge was Matthew Begbie, whose courage and fairness are remembered with gratitude to this day.

For years, Begbie patrolled the interior, often sleeping in a tent that had to double as his chambers. A giant of a man, he was not afraid to impose severe sentences if appropriate, even when his life was threatened. He is still referred to as 'the hanging judge' because he once condemned a white man to death for killing an Indian.

Begbie's influence still affects B.C.'s judiciary, for he headed it until his death in 1894. As always, the courts aim not merely to interpret the law but to see that justice is done, and that it is available to all. The judiciary is served by a progressive court system that covers the whole province.

B.C.'s senior court is the Court of Appeal, based in Vancouver, though it occasionally sits in Victoria. The court consists of nine justices appointed by the federal government. So are those of the B.C. Supreme Court, also based in Vancouver but regularly visiting Victoria, Prince George, and other centres on assize.

Then there are the county courts, which have intermediate jurisdiction in both civil and criminal matters. They too are served by justices appointed by Ottawa, who in this case live locally. Lesser cases are heard by judges of the provincial court, who are appointed by the province.

B.C.'s Supreme Court is housed not in Victoria but in Vancouver, where it occupies part of the provincial government complex at Robson Square.

Prince George is the capital of northern B.C., where this building holds branches of the provincial government and local courts.

capital city since 1850, which makes it senior to Ottawa. Victoria briefly lost its status in 1866 when Vancouver Island and mainland British Columbia were united with New Westminster as their capital. The slight was righted two years later when the legislature moved to the island.

As in other provinces, B.C.'s government is organized in three (some would say four) branches. The legislature makes law, the executive and administration put them into effect, and the judiciary interprets them. The areas of provincial jurisdiction are set out in the British North America Act passed in 1867.

The legislature consists of the lieutenant-governor (who represents the Crown) and 55 elected members. Besides passing laws, the members control the funds available to the administration and can call the executive to account for the manner in which it uses them.

The administration consists of some 16 departments, each responsible for a special area of government — for instance, education, health care, agriculture, or labour — and various Crown agencies. Each is headed or supervised by a member of the executive, who must answer for its activities in the legislature.

The executive is the lieutenant-governor-in-council — the council being the premier and his cabinet. The premier is the leader of the party with the largest representation, and in selecting his cabinet he takes account of geography, aiming to make sure that all regions have a say in cabinet deliberations.

Provincial governments are responsible for local administration, but in practice they delegate most of it to municipalities and other bodies who comprise a third level of government. In B.C. this level is split between municipalities and regional districts.

In general terms, the 28 regional districts are super-municipalities that between them cover the whole province except the sparsely populated northwest. They serve as umbrella organizations, providing the kind of services that can be shared by all the municipalities in their region — cities, districts, towns, and villages.

Individual municipalities are controlled by an elected council of a mayor and aldermen, and concentrate on purely local services. The regional districts are governed by a chairman and a board of directors, representing both their municipalities and the areas outside municipal boundaries.

The city hall in Dawson Creek in the Peace river country, the start of the Alaska Highway and one of the most northern communities in the province.

THE LEGISLATURE

In 1897 the whole British Empire celebrated Queen Victoria's diamond jubilee, nowhere more enthusiastically than in the city named after her. There, the palatial new quarters of the legislature were nearly ready for occupation.

The new building replaced 'the birdcages,' a trio of pagoda-like structures that had housed governments since 1859. In 1892 the B.C. legislature had invited architects all over Canada and the United States to submit plans for more impressive quarters, but eventually it opted for the work of Francis Rattenbury, an Englishman living locally.

The legislators hoped that the building would be in use during jubilee year. Even now, the canopy above the speaker's chair is dated '1897.' In the event, the builders were late, but that did not prevent the government from illuminating its new home from the outside.

To this day, the legislative building's illuminations startle visitors. In 1897 the effect was magical. There could have been no better symbol of British Columbia's booming prospects than the vast, domed structure surmounted by the golden statue of Captain George Vancouver.

Both inside and out, the legislative building seems larger than life, but the legislators and government officials who work there are by no means in awe of it. B.C.'s style of government is probably the most relaxed in Canada, based largely on word of mouth and close personal contact between the leaders.

In the past, British Columbians had a reputation for trusting a single individual with virtually unlimited power. That was particularly the case with W.A.C. Bennett, who for 20 years ran both the legislature and the administration as much by intuition as by listening to the advice of his colleagues.

B.C.'s legislature in session. Proceedings are ruled by the speaker, occupying the chair at the head of the chamber, and in front of him are the clerks of the house.

Now the government has become much larger, but even so the informality persists. It can be seen behind the scenes, as cabinet committees discuss policies and possible legislation. No minutes are kept, and in some committees government officials take part in discussions on a par with their ministers.

The informality can be seen even in the legislature, where in some cases the government officials join their ministers on the floor of the house. That is unheard of in the rest of Canada, but in British Columbia it makes sense to provide a minister with expert advice as he introduces legislation and copes with the taunts of the opposition.

Like everything else in B.C., politics are ruled by confrontation. The majority

The Premiers

Johnson

W. A. C. Bennett

Barrett

Bill Bennett

Before the turn of the century, B.C.'s legislature was controlled by groups rather than by parties. No fewer than 15 administrations took office between 1871 and 1903, some for no longer than a few months.

In 1903, Richard McBride formed the Conservative Party of British Columbia (C) and won the provincial election. McBride remained in office until 1915, by which time the pre-World War I boom was exhausted. In 1916 his party was ousted by the provincial Liberals (L).

The coalition of Liberals and Conservatives (coal) formed during World War II gave way to W.A.C. Bennett's Social Crediters (SC), who remained in power until 1972 when they were defeated by the New Democrats (NDP). The Social Crediters returned to office in 1975.

Here is a list of B.C.'s premiers since the province joined Confederation:

J.F. McCreight	1871–1872
Amor de Cosmos	1872–1874
G.A. Walkem	1974–1876
A.C. Elliott	1876–1878
G.A. Walkem	1878–1882
Robert Beaven	1882–1883
William Smithe	1883–1887
A.E.B. Davie	1887–1889
John Robson	1889–1892
Theodore Davie	1892–1895
J.H. Turner	1895–1898
C.A. Semlin	1898–1900

Joseph Martin	1900
James Dunsmuir	1900–1902
E.G. Prior	1902
Richard McBride (C)	1903–1915
W.J. Bowser (C)	1915–1916
H.C. Brewster (L)	1916–1918
John Oliver (L)	1918–1927
J.D. McLean (L)	1927–1928
S.F. Tolmie (C)	1928–1933
T.D. Pattullo (L)	1933–1941
John Hart (coal)	1941–1947
B.I. Johnson (coal)	1947–1952
W.A.C. Bennett (SC)	1952–1972
David Barrett (NDP)	1972–1975
Bill Bennett (SC)	1975–

of the province's voters are not committed to a party and are capable of swinging violently to the left (towards the New Democratic Party) or to the right (towards the Social Crediters). Liberals and Conservatives meekly occupy the middle ground.

Ironically, the Social Crediters and NDP have the same basic philosophy — that people need to be looked after and that society expects its government to provide a solid framework for all its activities. However, they approach their solutions from very different positions.

While in office between 1972 and 1975, the NDP passed more than 200 pieces of innovative legislation. In each, there was an assumption that what was good for the population as a whole must automatically be good for the individual, which left little room for alternatives but did promote a sense of community.

The Social Crediters, on the other hand, are committed to the individual and to keeping government at a respect-able arm's length from the society it serves. This was especially clear in 1979 when the Social Crediters began dismantling public corporations set up by the NDP. They planned to turn over the companies' assets to a private corporation in which all British Columbians might be given shares.

B.C.'s impressive legislative building in Victoria was first occupied in 1898, the year after Queen Victoria's diamond jubilee.

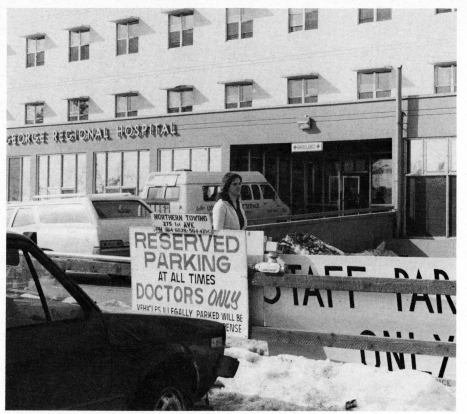

HEALTH CARE

The World Health Organization defines health as a state of 'complete physical, mental, social, and economic well-being, and not merely an absence of disease and infirmity.' That is a long-term goal, but in the short term, health authorities must aim to prevent, cure, or reduce avoidable suffering and handicap.

B.C.'s health care system rests on four pillars. One is the network of hospitals and institutions. Another is the provincial government, which provides most of the funding. The third is the medical profession and its ancillaries. The fourth is the education system, which trains doctors, nurses, and other personnel.

Some of the hospitals are owned and operated by the province, but

The regional hospital at Prince George, which is the chief health care facility in northern B.C.

Trustees and Physicians

As in so many areas of B.C. life, there is confrontation in the hospital system. On one side are the various hospital boards, who are legally responsible for what happens to their patients. On the other are the outside physicians who are granted hospital privileges.

Each of B.C.'s hospitals is control-

led by a board of trustees, some elected and some appointed. The elected trustees represent the hospital society, the people who have subscribed to the hospital corporation. The appointed trustees represent special interests like the B.C. ministry of health and the regional health district.

The role of hospital boards has changed dramatically since hospital

insurance was introduced. Before, hospitals were self-supporting, and a board spent much of its time raising funds. Today the funds come from the government, and the board's chief function is deciding how to allocate them.

A major portion of a hospital's budget is spent on equipment. In the past, boards tended to buy whatever equipment their physicians requested, without being sure that it was needed. As costs rose they began to ask questions, and have become far more knowledgeable about what goes on in their hospitals.

One result of this is they expect more from their physicians. In some hospitals, boards review their physicians' privileges every year, and there is no guarantee they will be renewed. Patients' best interests are being protected, and trustees once more wield the authority that is their due.

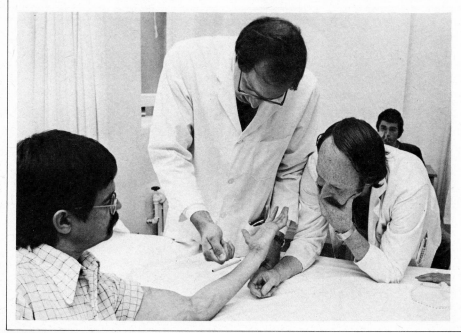

Physicians at a Vancouver hospital test the reflexes of an accident victim. Most physicians practise independently of a hospital, but use a hospital's facilities on being granted privileges by the board of trustees.

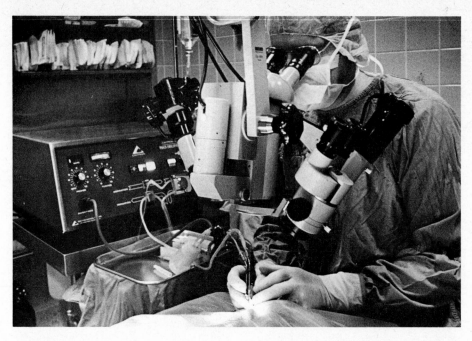

An eye surgeon undertakes a crucial operation under a microscope. One phenomenon of B.C. health care is that all its doctors practise inside the provincial medicare system.

most are autonomous corporations. The autonomous hospitals fall into three broad categories — small community hospitals offering primary care, larger regional hospitals providing primary and secondary care, and sophisticated referral centres that can handle exceptional cases.

Four of the province's five largest hospitals are in the lower mainland, among them the Vancouver General, which is by far the most important. The second largest is the Shaughnessy in Vancouver, then follow the Royal Jubilee in Victoria, the Lions Gate in North Vancouver, and the Burnaby General.

There are several specialized referral centres, among them children's hospitals in Vancouver and Victoria, and the Cancer Control Agency in Vancouver. The Royal Inland in Kamloops is the main referral centre for the interior, and the Prince George Regional has been expanded to serve the north.

It has usually been assumed that hospitals should provide the best care possible, regardless of expense. In the 1950s the provincial government introduced universal hospital insurance to help both hospitals and patients. In the 1960s it brought in universal medicare to cover the services of medical practitioners.

Unfortunately, costs have multiplied. Since the mid-1970s, the government has been looking for ways to save money. One obvious waste has been the length of time many patients have spent in hospital beds when less intensive nursing would have been adequate. Besides, many patients need not have entered hospital in the first place.

That is why the government has encouraged hospitals to place more emphasis on their outpatient clinics and on day-care surgery that allows patients to recover at home. The pro-

vince's public health service has been expanded so that nurses and physiotherapists can make home visits to patients who have been discharged early.

In the same vein, the government has extended health insurance to cover long-term care, whether at home or in institutions. The program is designed for those who cannot look after themselves but are not sick enough to need hospitalization — for instance, the aged, the mentally disturbed, and the physically handicapped.

Besides funding health care, the provincial government is responsible

for public health standards. Greater Vancouver and the Victoria region have their own health organizations, and the rest of the province is divided into 17 public health units. Their services range from maternal care to control of communicable diseases.

In treating mental illness, the province aims to use local resources. General hospitals are encouraged to offer psychiatric care, and some 30 mental health centres are staffed by experts. There are also several institutions for the mentally ill, emotionally disturbed, and senile who need inpatient care.

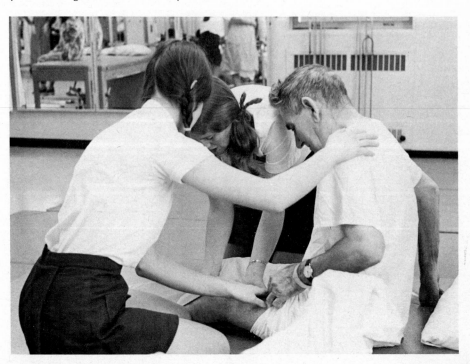

Physiotherapists help a patient to embark on his first walk after undergoing surgery.

The Universities

The idea of a provincial university was first put forward in 1877, but little happened until the University of British Columbia opened its doors in 1915. Its first quarters were on the site of the Vancouver General Hospital, but in 1925 work began on its present campus west of Vancouver's Stanley Park.

Today, the UBC campus is the largest in Canada and is also one of the most beautiful. The university contains 12 faculties and eight schools, among them those teaching agriculture, applied sciences (engineering), arts, commerce and business administration, education, forestry, law, medicine, nursing, and science.

Until 1963, UBC was by law the

Burnaby's Simon Fraser University was designed with an eye to student comfort. Students can walk between classes without being exposed to the elements.

province's only public university. Then the Universities Act was changed, and a college on Vancouver Island became the University of Victoria. The new university moved to its present campus in 1966, and its schools include political science, philosophy, economics, and mathematics.

A third university, Simon Fraser in Burnaby, was opened in 1965. Simon Fraser is different from the others in that it operates a trimester system. The academic year is divided into three self-contained units, and students enroll for one, two, or three semesters as they choose.

Simon Fraser has four faculties — arts, education, interdisciplinary studies, and science. Its impressive campus was designed by the Vancouver architect, Arthur Erickson. As yet, the only university in the interior is Notre Dame, a small private establishment in Nelson.

The special pride of the University of British Columbia in Vancouver is the Museum of Anthropology, designed by the local architect Arthur Erickson.

EDUCATION

When British Columbia joined Confederation in 1871, it had 21 schools — ten on the mainland, ten on Vancouver Island, and one on Saltspring Island. Most were single-room establishments staffed by an ill-paid teacher who concentrated on the 'three Rs.'

Today, there are schools all over the province — elementary, junior high, and high school. They are organized in 75 school districts and are controlled by elected boards of trustees that construct and maintain their buildings, hire teachers and other staff, decide attendance boundaries, and organize bus transportation.

In the past, school boards also decided what their schools should teach. Since 1977 they have had to follow a basic core curriculum laid down by the provincial education department, though they are encouraged to think of it as only a beginning and may supplement it with local material.

The core curriculum sets out the very least that a student should acquire at each stage of the school system. It covers skills of reading, writing, listening, speaking, math, measurement, science, social science, research, and even healthful living — all basics, but a far cry from the three Rs.

At first the curriculum covered only English-language instruction, but in 1978 an equivalent French curriculum was added. The Social Crediters wanted to offer parents a choice between English and French as their children's language of instruction, regardless of their background.

The first schools in B.C. were organized by clergy and therefore were denominational, but public schools have been non-sectarian since 1865. That is still the case today, but there are more than 150 'independent' schools that cater to special religious groups or offer special styles of teaching.

The independent schools are not controlled by the school boards, but subject to certain conditions, they do qualify for financial support from the province. In 1978 the Social Crediters increased the level of this support, with the idea of offering parents more choice in deciding how their children should be educated.

Beyond high school, the B.C. government has streamlined post-secondary education to eliminate dead ends. Two years at a community college can be complete in themselves or can lead straight into third year university, without the student having to start again.

B.C.'s first community college opened in 1969, and by 1979 there were 14 of them. Some operate storefront study centres in outlying communities. One even runs two mobile study centres, each equipped with a library and a laboratory, that visit fishing villages and logging camps.

Community colleges serve regions, but there are also specialist institutes that cater to the province as a whole. They include the Pacific Vocational Institute (training apprentices and journeymen), the Emily Carr College of Art, the Institute of Technology, and the Pacific Marine Training Institute, all in Vancouver.

Two newer ventures are the Justice Institute of British Columbia (which co-ordinates the various training programs in justice administration) and the Open Learning Institute. The latter is designed to carry post-secondary education to all parts of B.C. by mail and television.

Near Victoria is the Lester B. Pearson College of the Pacific, an international school opened in 1974 that combines academic pursuits with a wide range of physical and social activities. The college's staff and students are drawn from all over the world, and students work towards a diploma that is roughly the equivalent of first year university.

Recess at an elementary school in Prince Rupert. B.C.'s schools follow a core curriculum laid down by the provincial education department.

The Doukhobors

With help from the novelist Leo Tolstoy, 2000 members of a persecuted Christian sect left Russia in 1899 and settled in Saskatchewan. Known as the 'Spirit Wrestlers' or 'Doukhobors,' they were followed by 7400 more, but left 12 000 behind in Russia.

The Doukhobors were the most radical of a number of sects that had severed their ties with the Russian Orthodox church. Believing that the individual could relate to God directly, they rejected priests, churches, scriptures, rituals, and everything else that savoured of organized religion.

With hard work, the Doukhobors soon prospered in Saskatchewan. However, their beliefs and way of life were not welcomed, and in 1907, 600 of them left Saskatchewan for new land in the Kootenays. They were led by Peter Verigin, a mystic whom they regarded as divinely inspired.

The majority of the Doukhobors were ready to co-operate with the authorities, but an extremist group known as the Sons of Freedom thought differently. Insisting that God intended man to live naturally, they spurned money and the help of beasts of burden, and often paraded naked to demonstrate their purity and to advertise their views.

Doukhobors at prayer. The 'Freedomites,' who have become notorious for arson and nudity, represent only a tiny fraction of the denomination.

After Verigin died in 1912, relations between the Sons of Freedom and the orthodox Doukhobors steadily worsened. The Freedomites burned down property belonging to the orthodox, and the orthodox retaliated. The culprits were rounded up and brought to trial, but in court the Freedomites stripped to the buff in full view of all.

Between 1930 and the mid-1960s, many hundreds of Freedomites served prison terms for arson, destruction of property, or nudity. In most cases their targets were orthodox Doukhobors, but on occasions they attacked outsiders' property too — as in 1962 when they sabotaged the 3.5 km powerline that carried electricity across Kootenay Lake.

From the mid-1960s, it seemed that even the Freedomites were settling down and assimilating to the Canadian way of life. Then in 1977 came news of fresh arson involving rival Doukhobor factions. Once more Freedomites appeared in court, and once more they demonstrated their displeasure by taking off their clothes.

RELIGION

In the 1850s the Tsimshian of the north coast were not popular with their neighbours. They raided without mercy and enslaved the captives whom they did not slaughter. Worse, they were known to practise ritual cannibalism.

William Duncan, an Anglican missionary sent from Britain to convert the Tsimshian, saw clear evidence of the cannibalism soon after he arrived at Fort Simpson in 1857. Even so, he mastered the Tsimshian language and began travelling to their many villages with the message of the gospel.

Duncan was a lay missionary and by profession a schoolteacher. He found that both young Tsimshian and their elders were keen to learn to read and write, and by 1862 he had several hundred converts. To protect them from whisky and other bad influences, he led them to Metlakatla, an isolated village several kilometres from the site of Prince Rupert.

Many of Vancouver's East Indians worship at the Sikh temple, an impressive building that has become a focus of East Indian culture in the province.

Under Duncan's direction, the former cannibals developed a model settlement. They built houses, a school, and a large church, and supported themselves through a sawmill and a salmon cannery. Duncan taught his Tsimshian to spin, weave, make clothes, build furniture, play musical instruments, and take part in organized sports.

Metlakatla prospered until 1887, when Duncan fell out with his parent mission organization and with the bishop of New Caledonia. In protest, he moved the entire community about 150 km to the north-west, across the border into Alaska. There he ministered to 'New Metlakatla' until his death in 1918.

Duncan's settlement was unique, but even today there are missions active on B.C.'s northern coast. The Columbia Coastal Mission, an Anglican organization, co-operates with the United Church in operating vessels and aircraft that carry ministers to communities far away from conventional churches.

The Frontier Apostles are Roman Catholic lay brothers with headquarters in Prince George who serve Indian communities throughout the province. They follow in the footsteps of Oblate fathers who established mission stations in the Okanagan and on Vancouver Island in the 1840s and 1850s.

The great majority of British Columbians are Christians, but they belong to denominations that range from Lutheran to Pentecostal. Baptists, Mormons, Mennonites, Dutch Reformed, Salvation Army, and many more are represented. Each denomination has its own churches, and some have special schools and Bible colleges.

Churches apart, there is a Jewish community in Vancouver and elsewhere, and an active Buddhist following among those of Japanese or Chinese ancestry. Some Chinese Canadians are Taoists, the followers of Lao-tse, and some East Indians are Sikhs, monotheistic Hindus of whom the most orthodox still wear turbans in the tradition of their forefathers.

United Church worshippers emerge from a Sunday morning service in Vancouver. The United Church is one of the province's largest denominations, together with the Roman Catholic church and the Anglican church.

ARTISTS AND WRITERS

Few painters can write, and fewer writers can paint. Emily Carr of Victoria was an exception. Not only was she one of the most gifted and original painters that Canada has produced, but her books live on as classics of their kind.

Emily Carr was born in Victoria in 1871. She studied art in San Francisco and later in London and Paris, but her family did not approve of her work. Before going to Paris in 1910 she taught art in schools of the Vancouver area, but when she returned her paintings so shocked them that none would re-employ her.

Ignored by conventional society, Emily Carr took more pleasure in the woods and in the company of Indians. From an early stage she set out to paint the mystery of the rain forest and the timeless grandeur of forgotten totem poles, the last symbols of once-great Indian civilizations that were rapidly passing from view.

For 22 years Emily Carr kept a boarding-house to make ends meet, and for 15 of those years she did not paint. Then, during the 1920s her work was noticed by the anthropologist Marius Barbeau, and through him 50 of her paintings were exhibited at the National Gallery in Ottawa.

As a result of the exhibition, the painter met members of the Group of Seven, among them Lawren S. Harris, who encouraged her to work. In 1932 she became a founding member of the Canadian Group of Painters, and at least in Eastern Canada her work was recognized as something special.

During an illness Emily Carr wrote *Klee Wyck,* an autobiography that in 1941 won her the governor-general's prize for non-fiction. The achievement at last caught the interest of Victorian society, and the city honoured her with a seventieth birthday party.

Today, Emily Carr paintings are treasured in collections all over Canada. The largest group is housed at the Vancouver Art Gallery, but there is a problem. In her poverty, the artist used inferior materials, and many of her oils are literally fading away. The gallery has launched a major restoration appeal.

In B.C.'s arts world Emily Carr's work is in a class by itself, but other artists and writers have made important contributions. Some of them have been long-term residents, some only visitors, but each has thrown new light on B.C.'s special character.

A.Y. Jackson of the Group of Seven visited B.C. on a number of occasions and left many fine canvasses. Another member, Frederick Varley, lived and taught in Vancouver from 1926 until 1936, while Lawren S. Harris moved to Vancouver in 1930 and worked there until his death in 1940.

Both Varley and Harris worked closely with Jock MacDonald, an abstract painter who lived in B.C. between 1926 and 1945. Later he became a member of Toronto's Painters Eleven. Max Bates, the first Albertan to win national prominence as a painter, now lives in Victoria.

Jack Shadbolt is the best known of contemporary B.C. artists. This is his *Fetish*, painted in 1970.

Jack Shadbolt of Vancouver is probably the best known of B.C.'s contemporary artists. Once a student of Frederick Varley, he was for many years on the staff of the Vancouver School of Art. H. G. Glyde, until 1966 head of Fine Arts at the University of Alberta, is another fine painter who now lives in B.C.

The province's writers include George Woodcock of Vancouver, whose many books include critical studies and philosophical works; Bruce Hutchison of Victoria, a journalist who has won three governor-general's awards for non-fiction; and Barry Broadfoot of Vancouver, another journalist who has made a name as an oral historian.

Malcolm Lowry, an English-born novelist, lived in a simple shack near Vancouver between 1939 and 1954. There he completed his masterpiece *Under the Volcano,* a testimony of his earlier experiences in Mexico when in the grip of alcohol, as well as stories and other works set in B.C.

Playwright Carol Bolt grew up in Vancouver, and novelist Margaret Laurence lived there for years. Both are now in Ontario. Jack Hodgins lives near Nanaimo and writes about Vancouver Island. Eric Nicol of Vancouver writes humour, and B.C.'s poets include Earle Birney of Vancouver and Susan Musgrave of Vancouver Island.

Some of the writers and artists now prominent in B.C. and elsewhere in Canada were once members of Intermedia, an exciting arts organization that flourished in Vancouver during the 1960s. Painters, sculptors, writers, musicians, performing artists, and many more shared in its workshops, exhibitions, and performances.

Intermedia's many disciplines have gone their separate ways, and some of the artists are now members of 'parallel galleries' — communal workshops that provide outlets not available through commercial galleries. Victoria has the Open Space, and Vancouver has the

National Gallery of Canada

Emily Carr's Memalilaqua, Knight Inlet **was painted in 1912, long before the artist became famous.**

Western Front and Pumps and Power.

Each of the parallel galleries is run by and for artists, and offers exhibitions and concerts for its members. Painting, sculpture, modern music and jazz, photography, dance, and video screenings are all featured.

PERFORMANCES

Vancouver's first Orpheum was opened in 1914, a vaudeville-cum-movie house that was the city's leading attraction for years. In 1927 a 'new' Orpheum was built on Granville Street, seating nearly 3000 and replete with 100 chandeliers, ornate columns, and a massive dome six stories above the main floor.

The new theatre was the marvel of the city and became the showplace, not only of vaudeville, but of all the arts. From 1930 it was the home of the newly formed Vancouver Symphony Orchestra and remained so until 1959, when the symphony moved to the multi-purpose Queen Elizabeth Playhouse.

By then, vaudeville was on its last legs, and the Orpheum concentrated on films. Responding to a new vogue, in 1972 its owners planned to convert the building into a number of small cinemas. Civic groups protested at the loss of such a fine auditorium, and the developers agreed to sell the Orpheum to the city.

Seven million dollars were spent on refurbishing the building, and in 1977 it was reopened as the permanent home of the Vancouver Symphony. Once more it stands as a symbol of all the performing arts, the largest concert hall in Canada and one of the most elegant in North America.

In the Orpheum the Vancouver Symphony performs the 13 concerts of its annual main series, all of which are broadcast by the CBC, and five mini-series concerts too. Its season extends from September to the end of June, and the orchestra has a subscription list of 40 000 — one of North America's largest.

Frequently the symphony performs with choral groups, notably the Vancouver Bach Choir, which was also founded in 1930. Each spring the Bach Choir joins forces with the Chamber Choir (one of only two professional choirs in Canada), the Cantata Singers, and the Gallery Singers, to present a four-choirs festival.

The symphony also plays for visiting ballet companies and for the Vancouver Opera Association, which builds its productions around a small core of resident professionals. As yet there is no fully professional ballet company in the province, but Pacific Ballet Theatre is gaining strength.

Of course, there is much musical

Christopher Newton plays Malvolio in a Vancouver Playhouse production of Shakespeare's *Twelfth Night.* **The company is the only one in Canada that has its own theatre school.**

activity outside Vancouver. New Westminster and Delta (the sprawling municipality south of Vancouver) both have symphony orchestras. So have the Okanagan, Kamloops, Prince George (the New Caledonia), and Nanaimo.

The Victoria Symphony is well supported at home and makes a specialty of touring. In addition there are several chamber orchestras and ensembles, among them the Purcell String Quartet based in Vancouver. Simon Fraser University and the University of Victoria are noted for experimental music.

Modern dance attracts enthusiastic audiences in B.C., and the Anna Wyman Dance Theatre of Vancouver is one of the leading troupes in Canada. The Paula Ross Dancers are well supported too, and other groups include Prism Dance Theatre, Mountain Dance Theatre, Fulcrum, and Terminal City Dance, all of the Vancouver area.

To survive, the professional dance troupes must tour both inside and outside the province. So must many of

Vancouver's Orpheum theatre is once more the home of the Vancouver Symphony Orchestra.

B.C.'s professional theatre companies. Caravan Stage, which winters in the Okanagan, spends its summers travelling through B.C. and Alberta in a gypsy caravan towed by a Clydesdale.

There are professional companies in Victoria, Kamloops, Fort St. John (children's theatre), and the West Kootenay, but inevitably most are in the lower mainland. Vancouver holds at least 12 professional companies, among them the Playhouse Theatre, which has its own theatre school.

The Playhouse company was launched in 1962, and each year presents a main series of five plays at the Queen Elizabeth Playhouse. In spite of adopting the name, the theatre company does not control the Playhouse and must share the facilities with the other groups that rent them.

Besides the main series, Playhouse Theatre presents a 'new series' of plays at Spratt's Ark. As the west coast's chief regional theatre, the Playhouse prefers to import directors rather than players, and actors are drawn from the resident company — among them students from the theatre school.

The Playhouse's season is supposed to cater to many tastes, but the Arts Club Theatre of Granville Island is deliberately commercial. Tamahnous Theatre is one of several groups that perform their own material, and Westcoast Actors provide alternatives even to the alternate.

Tamahnous Theatre is based at the Vancouver East Cultural Centre, one of a number of community cultural centres created by local arts associations. Some are housed in resurrected buildings, among them a firehall in Gastown and an old armoury in Kimberley, and nearly all act as entrepreneurs in bringing touring groups to their regions.

Judith Forst, originally from New Westminster and now known internationally, sings in Vancouver Opera's production of Bizet's *Carmen.* **With her is the chorus, all Vancouverites.**

The Professionals

In 1954 the British Commonwealth was still an empire, and the Empire Games were held in Vancouver. The city built the Empire Stadium to accommodate the games' track and field events, and opened the door to major-league professional sport.

Soon after the games ended, the stadium was filled for the first appearance of the B.C. Lions football team, a franchise in the Canadian Football League. As years passed, the team improved its performance, until in 1964 it beat the Hamilton Tiger-Cats and won the Grey Cup.

Professional hockey was introduced to Vancouver as early as 1911. In 1914-1915 the Vancouver Millionaires won the Stanley Cup. However, interest in professional hockey waned until the building of the Pacific Coliseum in 1968. A year later a local minor league club, the Vancouver Canucks, was admitted to the National Hockey League.

The Canucks and Lions have loyal followings, but close on their heels is Vancouver's newest professional franchise, a soccer team. The Vancouver Whitecaps joined the North American Soccer League in 1974, and like the Lions they play in the Empire Stadium.

Professional rodeo has long been popular in the interior. Rodeos are an annual event from Williams Lake to Cranbrook, and B.C. has produced many Canadian champions. Not to be outdone, in the late 1960s the men of the woods devised a rodeo of their own, based on logging sports.

Like rodeo, logging sports emerge

Logging sports devised in B.C. have become so popular that some loggers have become professional athletes. One event is chainsaw bucking, in which the competitor must perch on the log that he is sawing.

from a work situation. Events include springboard chopping, peavy log rolling, axe throwing, and powersaw bucking. The climax of a logging event is a relay race involving teams of six. Each man completes an allotted task based on his specialty event, then hands on to the next.

In spite of their short history, logging sports have become popular throughout British Columbia and in the western United States. Some loggers have become full-time sportsmen, honing their skills in pursuit of a world championship and providing magnificent entertainment at the same time.

SPORT AND FITNESS

Other Canadians have long been convinced that British Columbians are half crazy. As if to prove the point, each summer a large flotilla of powered bathtubs speeds across the Georgia Strait from Nanaimo to Vancouver.

Nanaimo's bathtub race began as a joke in 1967, but now attracts serious competitors from as far away as Australia. Even so, no cash prizes are awarded. For bathtubbers, the goal is not so much to win as to finish the course, for that is an achievement in itself.

Bathtubbing is just one of a score of sports that take advantage of British Columbia's salt water. Islands included, the province has a coastline of more than 27 000 km. Marinas and boat harbours abound in the Vancouver area, Victoria, and for much of the way up the Georgia Strait.

Vancouver, in fact, has the largest concentration of pleasure craft in Canada. Many of them are powered, used for fishing or towing water-skiers. The others are sailboats, whether cruising yachts, dinghies, or the sleek ocean racers that enjoy major challenges like Victoria's Swiftsure Classic.

Next to the sea and inland waters like the Okanagan lakes, British Columbia's greatest recreational asset is its mountains. Hiking and trail-riding are the sports for summer, and downhill skiing for winter, particularly at premier resorts like those in the Kootenays and Whistler Mountain, which is only 120 km from Vancouver.

The Grouse Mountain ski resort actually overlooks Vancouver, but serious skiers complain that its snow is too wet. Even so, Vancouver is one of the few places in the world where a snow skier high on the slopes can look down and watch a water-skier far below him.

Grouse Mountain has achieved fame of another kind among hang-gliders. It is reputed to be one of the world's best launching-sites, as is a spot overlooking Nelson in the Selkirks. Those who want to fall from even greater heights take up sky-diving, which is another sport with a large following.

Down to earth, British Columbia has its fair share of conventional sports. Tennis, golf, and swimming are well

represented. There are 100 000 horse-owners in the province, and show-jumping is big. Some of those who do not ride pitch horseshoes instead, a sport now recognized at the provincial games.

Hockey and basketball are the most popular team sports, but soccer is catching up with them at the expense of football. The aristocrat, however, is box

A skier in Cypress provincial park on Vancouver's north shore has a fine view of Howe Sound and the Coastal mountains in the distance.

lacrosse. British Columbian teams have won the Mann Cup, Canada's senior amateur lacrosse trophy, on more than 40 occasions since it was presented in 1910.

71

WILDLIFE

British Columbians share their province with a rich diversity of wildlife. From wave-swept rocks off the Queen Charlotte islands to the depths of the rain forest, there are habitats to suit most of the creatures that make their home in Canada.

Some of the creatures are spectacular. Grizzly bears roam the mountains and other wilderness areas of the mainland. Black bears are found in all parts of the province, including Vancouver Island. The Kermode, a white mutant of the black bear, is restricted to the Prince Rupert region.

Cougar are found on the mainland south of the Skeena and Peace rivers, and on Vancouver Island, too. Packs of timber wolves hunt in the forests. There are goats high in the mountains, and wild sheep as well — bighorns south of the Peace river, thinhorns (Dall and Stone) to the north.

Roosevelt elk are native to Vancouver Island, but have now been reintroduced to the mainland. Rocky Mountain elk are found in the Kootenays and in the foothills of the Peace river area. There are mule deer over most of the interior, whitetailed deer in the southeast, and blacktailed deer on the coast.

Most of the species typical of Canada's northern forest are well represented in British Columbia, though a century ago moose rarely ventured south of the Prince George region. Logging operations opened the forest, and moose steadily extended their range so that now it approaches the United States border.

The islands' western and northern coasts are favourite haunts of seals and sea lions, and sea otters have been re-established. There are also 15 species of seabirds, many of them found nowhere else in Canada. The seabirds nest in colonies that can be visited only by boat, and all are protected.

Inland, there is a dazzling variety of birds, some migratory and some permanent residents. The migratory species are mostly waterfowl — black brants,

A fine specimen of a bighorn ram, high in the mountains south of the Peace river. North of the river is thinhorn country.

The cougar's range extends across Canada, but the species is most plentiful on Vancouver Island.

Canada and snow geese, trumpeter and whistling swans, and a host of brightly plumaged ducks from spoonbills to baldpates and from sprigtails to butterballs.

Upland game birds include three species of ptarmigan, four species of grouse, and species of partridge and pheasant introduced from Europe and China. Among the non-game species are 34 birds of prey, among them bald and golden eagles, peregrine falcons, marsh hawks, and great horned owls.

A colony of sea lions plays in the water off Vancouver Island's west coast. B.C. provides suitable habitats for a wide range of fauna, and they are among the province's special prides.

Mystery Monsters

Like Scotland's Loch Ness, the Okanagan has a monster. British Columbians named it Ogopogo after a British music hall song, but local Indians have long known it as N'ha-a-itk, meaning 'holy serpent of the water.'

Stories of the serpent have circulated for at least three centuries. Like its Loch Ness counterpart, Ogopogo has been described as long and humped, undulating when swimming and occasionally raising its head from the water. Recent sightings have been so numerous that most local people believe the monster exists.

In spite of the attention, Ogopogo seems to be benign. Indians used to tell terrible stories of Ogopogo's anger, but there have been no reports of a violent attack in more than a century. Indeed, Ogopogo seems to crave company, and has often been reported swimming near populated areas.

Another monster frequently sighted in British Columbia is the Sasquatch, a hairy humanoid said by Indians to be descended from a race of giants. Both male and female Sasquatches have been described, and according to most reports, both sexes are abnormally tall and have ape-like limbs.

Remains of a long-extinct race of giants were found in Mexico in the 1930s, and some paleontologists are prepared to believe that Sasquatches exist. Whether they are real or imagined, reports agree that the creatures are extremely strong, live in caves, and communicate with each other through bird-like whistles.

THE PARKS

Among British Columbia's brightest jewels are five national parks and more than 300 provincial parks. Some of them are world famous, some scarcely known even by local people, but together they conserve a major segment of B.C.'s heritage.

In total, the parks cover nearly five million hectares, but even that amounts to less than four per cent of B.C.'s surface area. Most of the parks are in alpine or sub-alpine regions that could not be used for anything else. Only small areas have any agricultural potential, and the forest value is minimal.

The five national parks are Yoho, Kootenay, Glacier, Mount Revelstoke, and Pacific Rim. Yoho (1886, 1313 km²) and Kootenay (1920, 1406 km²) are in the Rockies, and share common boundaries with each other and with Banff National Park across the mountains. Yoho contains the spectacular Tokakkaw Falls, and Kootenay holds the Vermilion valley.

Glacier (1886, 1349 km²) is set in the Selkirk and Purcell mountains, and contains more than 100 spectacular rivers of ice. Special crews control scores of avalanche zones that overlook the Trans-Canada highway. Mount Revelstoke (1914, 263 km²) shares the Selkirks and is flanked by the Monashee mountains.

These four parks are similar in that they are all in the mountains. Pacific Rim (1970, 389 km²), however, is a marine park on Vancouver Island's west coast. Centred on Long Beach, one of the few stretches of sand along the B.C. shore, the park contains the West Coast Trail and many islands, too.

B.C.'s provincial parks show much more variety than do the national parks. Most are small, but about 30 of them cover more than 150 km². Some — Mount Robson and Mount Assiniboine, for instance — are often mistaken for

Lake O'Hara Lodge, a special retreat in Yoho National Park. Yoho is one of four national mountain parks in the province, not counting several provincial parks.

Climbers add their names to a list of those who have scaled Castor Peak in Glacier National Park. The list is deposited in a cairn at the summit.

Long Beach in Pacific Rim National Park, one of the few sandy stretches on Vancouver Island's west coast.

national parks, and at least 20 of them contain features of national significance.

The oldest provincial park is Strathcona (1911, 2270 km²) at the heart of Vancouver Island. Its lakes, mountains, and wildlife are spectacular in all seasons. The island contains more than 40 other provincial parks, among them offshore islands, beaches, falls, forests, lakes, and wilderness areas.

On the mainland, there are several huge wilderness regions that hold nature conservancy areas, where the works of man are not allowed. Tweedsmuir (900 km²) in the west-central region, Spatzisi Plateau in the north-west, and Wells Gray (5200 km²) in the Cariboo are all in this category.

Mount Robson (2172 km²) contains the highest mountain in the Canadian Rockies, and adjoins Jasper National Park across Alberta's boundary. Garibaldi (1920 km²) is centred on Mount Garibaldi in the Coastal range, and with its neighbour Golden Ears (594 km²) is easily accessible from Vancouver.

Kokanee Glacier and Top of the World in the Kootenays, Bowron Lake in the Cariboo, Muncho Lake on the Alaska highway — there are provincial parks all over the province. The most remote is Mount Edziza in the Tahltan highlands, a volcano that erupted as recently as four centuries ago.

Bird watchers head for the Mitlenatch Island sanctuary, canoeists traverse Bowron Lake's water circuit, alpine or nordic skiers make use of winter facilities at parks like Manning. Backpackers, trail riders, and indeed all who love and respect nature are welcome at sites throughout the province.

The chief purpose of national parks is to conserve natural features. Provincial parks are created to serve the needs of British Columbians. Local people comprise 60 per cent of park users, while 20 per cent are from elsewhere in Canada and 20 per cent are from other countries, particularly the United States.

Kootenay National Park holds the Radium hot springs, a health spa that attracts visitors in all seasons.

Living History

Besides nature parks, the national and provincial systems contain several special historic parks that bring the past to life. One of them is a re-creation of Fort Langley in the lower mainland, a fur-trading post established in 1827.

During the 1850s Fort Langley became the starting point for the Fraser river gold rush, and for a brief period in 1858 it was B.C.'s capital. From that time the fort slipped into decline, but some of its original buildings survive and others have been reconstructed to show how Fort Langley looked in its heyday.

Fort Rodd Hill, a coastal artillery station outside Victoria, is the only other national historic park in B.C. Erected between 1895 and 1900, its defences are still intact. Fort Steele near Cranbook, built around the province's first mounted police post, is a 'living museum' that recreates Kootenay life of the period 1890 to 1905.

The most exciting of the historic parks is Barkerville in the Cariboo. When restoration began in 1958, only 15 of Barkerville's original buildings were still standing, but hotels, churches, and saloons have been added. Each summer costumed attendants play the roles of pioneers as they show what life was like between 1869 and 1885.

ENVIRONMENT

With much of the world's most beautiful scenery on their doorsteps, British Columbians have a vested interest in their environment. Clean air and clean water are at the roots of their lifestyle, and they are constantly on guard against the threat of pollution.

Compared with Eastern Canadians, they have escaped lightly. In the past, heavy industries like smelters and pulpmills discharged poisonous effluents, power dams interrupted salmon rivers, and mines and logging operations scarred the landscape. Yet the province as a whole was only minimally affected.

Of course, there have been disasters. One of the worst occurred in 1913 and 1914, when railroad workers dumped large amounts of debris into the Fraser river at Hell's Gate canyon. A landslide completed the effect and the river was blocked. The world-famous run of sockeye salmon was permanently crippled.

The river was partially reopened in 1915, and ingenious ladder fishways helped fish to overcome the obstacle. Similar fishways have been installed elsewhere in the Fraser system, and the temptation to build large hydroelectric dams in the valley has been resisted. Perhaps the Hell's Gate tragedy has been beneficial.

Another story of pollution put to rights involves the lead-zinc smelter at Trail. Before 1930, the smelter gave off noxious sulphur dioxide that destroyed the vegetation for many kilometres around. Then scientists found a way to make sulphuric acid from the gas, and the pollution count dropped overnight. Trees and grass were planted, and today Trail shows little evidence of the moonscape that once surrounded it.

Industries are one potential source of pollution, municipalities another. Garbage and sewage disposal have caused problems in the past and are now subject to strict pollution controls exercised by the provincial government. Be-

sides, throughout the province there is special vigilance over water quality.

One of the most controversial problems has occurred in the Okanagan. There, fertilizer washed into the lakes from orchards on the hillsides has encouraged the spread of Eurasian milfoil, a weed that threatens to choke the lakes and ruin their recreational value.

Much of the weed is being removed by machine, but to destroy it permanently the province is using a herbicide, 2,4-D. The government insists that 2,4-D is environmentally safe and will not harm fish, birds, or other wildlife, much less poison drinking water. But there are other opinions, and the Okanagan has been the scene of fiery confrontations between government officials and protesting environmentalists.

Trail's smelter used to make it one of B.C.'s eyesores, but determined efforts have cut down pollution and helped to heal the scars of the past.

Greenpeace

There is no shortage of environmental groups in B.C., but one of them is famous. The Greenpeace Foundation of Vancouver makes a specialty of challenging some of the world's most powerful governments, and its bold tactics have produced a string of convincing victories.

Greenpeace had its start in the anti-nuclear crusades of the 1960s. In 1969 a committee was formed in Vancouver to protest American underground testing in the Aleutians, which, it was feared, would set off a tidal wave. In 1971 the committee chartered a fishing vessel to enter the testing zone.

The vessel was renamed *Greenpeace* to reflect both environmental and anti-bomb concerns. It came close to the Aleutians, but was forced to turn back when the test was postponed. Meanwhile, an old minesweeper renamed *Greenpeace 2* set sail for the test, but failed to reach it in time because it was delayed by bad weather.

The test went ahead, though to Vancouverites' glee the Americans cancelled the rest of their program. The two protest voyages had aroused passionate enthusiasm in Vancouver. In 1972 funds were raised to send *Greenpeace 3*, a sailing ketch, to interrupt the French nuclear tests being staged east of Tahiti.

In spite of *Greenpeace 3*, the French exploded their device, and the protesters escaped nuclear fallout only because the wind was blowing the other way. A French minesweeper later rammed the yacht and crippled it, but the next year it was back on the testing grounds as *Greenpeace 4* — until boarded by the French and forcibly ejected.

The Greenpeace movement was now international, particularly as Vancouverite environmentalists had invaded Paris to publicize their cause. Not entirely by coincidence, the Gaullist government was toppled and the nuclear tests were abandoned. Meanwhile, the foundation turned its attention to a new problem, the hunt for whales.

At the time, whales seemed perilously close to extinction. Japanese and Russian fleets pursued them to the ends of the earth, and the International Whaling Commission seemed powerless to protect them. In summer 1975, *Greenpeace 5* and 6 (the fishing boat and the ketch) sailed from Vancouver

Greenpeacers in a rubber dinghy cross the bows of a Russian whaling ship and hinder it from pursuing its prey. In the distance is *Greenpeace*, **the converted minesweeper** *James Bay*.

to 'Save the Whales.'

After eight weeks' search, *Greenpeace 5* sighted a Russian factory ship off the California coast. Greenpeacers manned rubber rafts and came between the Russians and their prey — but in vain, as a harpoon sped overhead and killed a whale while they watched. The film they took shocked audiences worldwide.

Since the first encounter, Greenpeace has used converted minesweepers to harass the whalers, and in 1978 for the first time there was no whaling east of Hawaii. Now the battle has entered the Atlantic. The Save the Whale campaign has won support for Greenpeace from all over the world.

Today, Greenpeace is an international organization active in environmental issues from budworm spraying to the Newfoundland seal fishery, with chapters all over North America and in many other countries. Its courageous, non-violent confrontations have been widely copied, but at heart it is still a phenomenon special to Vancouver.

'KSAN

During the 1960s, Gitksan Indians of the Hazelton area built a small replica of a traditional longhouse beside the highway to Prince Rupert. There they sold local artifacts and handcrafts and did so well that they decided to re-create a whole Indian village as a tourist attraction.

The result is 'Ksan, not merely a living museum but a symbol of Indian aspirations throughout the north-west. Nobody lives in 'Ksan's six houses, but they are the pride of some 5000 local Indians who are giving new life to the ancient skills inherited from their forefathers.

'Ksan is located on the Skeena river, where a tributary creates a peninsula. It was opened to the public in 1969, and each of its houses serves a different purpose. In one, the Frog House of the Distant Past, visitors are shown how Indians lived from the land before the advent of white men.

The recreated village of 'Ksan, near Hazelton on the Skeena river. Totem poles front six houses that showcase Gitksan history and heritage.

The Wolf House of the Grandfathers shows how local lifestyles changed through the introduction of trade goods. The house is organized as if for a feast, and once a week during the season the 'Ksan Dancers perform songs and rituals used with the permission of the chiefs to whom they belong.

The dancers' elaborate costumes are made and stored in the house of Masks and Robes, where seamstresses and weavers are at work. Carvers are in the Carving House of All Time. Their work and that of craftsmen elsewhere in the region is displayed in the Today House of the Arts.

The sixth house, the Fireweed House of Treasure, is used to display the ceremonial regalia of local chiefs. Like the others, it is decorated with carved interior poles and elaborately painted screens. Since its foundation, 'Ksan's fame has spread far beyond B.C.'s boundaries and it has become a shrine of the Indian renaissance.

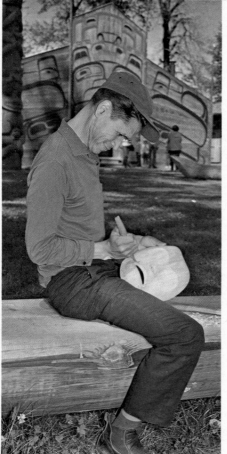

All B.C.'s coastal tribes have proud traditions of craftsmanship. Here a Gitksan carver works on a mask.

Photograph Credits

Alcan Aluminum: p. 33 bottom; *Beautiful British Columbia:* p. 6, p. 14, p. 34, p. 36, p. 51 top, p. 52, p. 58, p. 59 bottom, p. 64 top, p. 70, p. 71, p. 78 top and bottom; *British Columbia Dept. of Agriculture:* p. 26, p. 27 top and bottom; *British Columbia Dept. of Economic Development:* p. 39 top and bottom; *British Columbia Ferry Corp.:* p. 24 top, p. 46 top and bottom; *British Columbia Forest Products:* p. 38 top; *British Columbia Forest Service:* p. 28 top and bottom, p. 29 top and bottom, p. 30, p. 31 top and bottom; *British Columbia Hydro:* p. 42, p. 43 top and bottom; *British Columbia Railway:* p. 45 bottom; *Humphry Clinker:* p. 38 bottom, p. 40 bottom, p. 44, p. 50 top and bottom, p. 51 bottom, p. 53 top and bottom, p. 55 top and bottom, p. 56 top and bottom, p. 57 top and bottom, p. 60 top; *Cominco Ltd.:* p. 76; *Environment Canada:* p. 37 top and bottom; *Government of the Yukon:* p. 45 top; *Greenpeace Foundation:* p. 77; *Kaiser Resources:* p. 35 top and bottom; *National Air Photo Library:* p. 4 bottom; *Ontario Heritage Foundation:* p. 66, p. 67; *Parks Canada:* (R. D. Muir) p. 5 top, (W. Wyett) p. 5 bottom, (P. McCloskey) p. 7 bottom, (T. W. Hall) p. 73 top, p. 73 bottom, (Blair Stevens) p. 74 top, (John G. Woods) p. 74 bottom, (G. E. Tayler) p. 75 top, (P. McCloskey) p. 75 bottom; *Penny Parsons:* p. 3, p. 41, p. 62 top and bottom, p. 63, p. 64 bottom; *Placer Development:* p. 25 top, p. 32 top and bottom, p. 33 top; *Port of Vancouver:* p. 47, p. 48 top and bottom, p. 49; *Provincial Archives of British Columbia:* p. 8 top, p. 13 bottom, p. 15 top and bottom, p. 16 top and bottom, p. 17 top and bottom, p. 18 top, p. 19 top, p. 24 bottom; *Jim Ryan:* p. 54; *Vancouver General Hospital:* p. 40 top, p. 60 bottom, p. 61 top and bottom; *Vancouver Opera Assoc.:* (John Helcermanas) p. 69 bottom; *Vancouver Playhouse:* (David Cooper) p. 68; *Vancouver Symphony Orchestra:* p. 69 top.

Acknowledgments

Many individuals, corporations, institutions, and government departments assisted us in gathering information and illustrations. Among them we owe special thanks to the following:

Air Canada
Alcan Canada
Aimée Anglin
George Baker
Beautiful British Columbia
Diane Bell
B. C. Chamber of Commerce
B. C. Department of Agriculture
B. C. Department of the Attorney-General
B. C. Department of Economic Development
B. C. Department of Education
B. C. Department of the Environment
B. C. Department of Finance
B. C. Department of Health
B. C. Department of Highways
B. C. Department of Labour
B. C. Department of Mines and Petroleum Resources
B. C. Department of Municipal Affairs and Housing
B. C. Department of Recreation and Conservation
B. C. Department of the Travel Industry
B. C. Executive Council
B. C. Ferry Corporation

B. C. Fish and Wildlife Branch
B. C. Forest Products
B. C. Forest Service
B. C. Hydro
B. C. Packers
B. C. Parks Branch
B. C. Provincial Museum
B. C. Railway
B. C. Touring Council
Canadian Government Office of Tourism
Cominco Limited
Council of Forest Industries of B.C.
Crown Zellerbach
Emily Carr College of Art
Environment Canada
Peter Faun
Fisheries Association of B.C.
Greenpeace Foundation
Geological Survey of Canada
Carl Jones
Kaiser Resources
Al and Sharon McKinnon

Rod Marining
Elaine Maxymyshyn
Kathy Meiklejohn
National Photography Collection
Penny Parsons
Ralph Pettie
Placer Development
Playhouse Theatre Company
Port of Vancouver
Public Archives Canada
Simon Fraser University
Sport B.C.
Christine Thompson
University of British Columbia
Vancouver Art Gallery
Vancouver Canucks
Vancouver General Hospital
Vancouver Opera Association
Vancouver Symphony Orchestra
Vancouver Whitecaps
Weyerhaeuser Canada
Western Front

Canadian Cataloguing in Publication Data

Hocking, Anthony, 1944-
   British Columbia

(Canada series)

Includes index.
ISBN 0-07-082690-0

1. British Columbia.   2. British Columbia —
Description and travel.   I. Series.

FC3811.6.H63   971.1   C77-001608-1
F1087.5.H63

1 2 3 4 5 6 7 8 9 10 BP 8 7 6 5 4 3 2 1 0 9

Printed and bound in Canada

Index